T0121265

How to Choose the Perfect School:

What 21st Century Parents Need to Know about K-12 Education

Mary Lang, Ed.D.

Designer: Melissa Rockwood.
Contact the author at: mary@schoolchoiceadvisors.com

Order this book online at www.trafford.com/05-0538
or email orders@trafford.com

Most Trafford titles are also available at major online book retailers.

© Copyright 2007 Mary Lang.
All rights reserved. No part of this publication may be reproduced, stored in a retrieval
system, or transmitted, in any form or by any means, electronic, mechanical, photocopying,
recording, or otherwise, without the written prior permission of the author.

Note for Librarians: A cataloguing record for this book is available from Library
and Archives Canada at www.collectionscanada.ca/amicus/index-e.html

Printed in Victoria, BC, Canada.

ISBN: 978-1-4120-5640-3

*We at Trafford believe that it is the responsibility of us all, as both individuals
and corporations, to make choices that are environmentally and socially sound.
You, in turn, are supporting this responsible conduct each time you purchase a
Trafford book, or make use of our publishing services. To find out how you are
helping, please visit www.trafford.com/responsiblepublishing.html*

*Our mission is to efficiently provide the world's finest, most comprehensive
book publishing service, enabling every author to experience success.
To find out how to publish your book, your way, and have it available
worldwide, visit us online at www.trafford.com/10510*

Trafford PUBLISHING™ www.trafford.com

North America & international
toll-free: 1 888 232 4444 (USA & Canada)
phone: 250 383 6864 ♦ fax: 250 383 6804 ♦ email: info@trafford.com

The United Kingdom & Europe
phone: +44 (0)1865 722 113 ♦ local rate: 0845 230 9601
facsimile: +44 (0)1865 722 868 ♦ email: info.uk@trafford.com

10 9 8 7 6 5 4

In loving memory of my father who devoted his life to caring for children.

Author's Notes

For over 25 years, I have been interacting with and listening to parents as a teacher, parent, and as a developer and administrator of educational programs. As my own children continue to go through various developmental stages, I hear the messages and concerns of parents more clearly and on many different levels.

The purpose of this book is to assist parents in realizing the importance of their educational choices and contemplating the effects that these choices will make on their child's future. Even if parents do not agree with my message, I hope that this book will stimulate their thinking and their understanding of the impact that making good educational choices has on their child's ability to fulfill his/her potential.

Acknowledgements

My gratitude to the individuals who have supported my writing:

Julie Monroe, suburb editor, visionary and champion of this project.

Joe Thompson, my husband, fellow educator, and part-time editor, whose dedicated insight and contributions helped me shape and achieve the educational programs I have developed.

Melissa Rockwood, extraordinary artist and cover designer, who creates the designs to support my writings.

Dylan and Quinn Thompson, my children, who are my reason for being passionate about education.

Betty Lang, my mother, who has offered me continuous encouragement throughout the project.

Teachers, students, parents and administrators at the Moscow Charter School for teaching me many of the lessons I have learned about education.

Table of Contents

Chapter 1:
A Parent/Educator's Perspective on School Choice – 5

Parents should understand their own personal philosophy about education and then set goals for their child before choosing a school. Parents can learn from my perspective and experiences as an educator and parent. They will be encouraged to be creative in designing their child's long-term educational program and supplementing traditional programs with alternative programming.

Chapter 2:
From Bobbitt to Bush: Has Anything Changed? – 11

Traditional public school curricula are not much different than they were 100 years ago. Now as then, standardized curricula, rote learning, and conformity are predominate features of most public schools. Over the past century there have some attempts at change, but the system will not allow it. Current developments in education, such as the federal No Child Left Behind Act that mandates standardized testing as the single measure of student academic achievement, is an example. Charter schools and vouchers may be the vanguard of permanent and substantial change.

Chapter 3:
Brain-Based Learning – 19

Groundbreaking research on the learning brain has occurred over the past 20 years. Features of a learning environment that take knowledge of the learning brain in mind are defined and described. These features include critical periods of learning, stimulating multiple senses, the importance of early enrichment, the role of emotion in learning, learning styles, relaxation, movement, and mentoring.

Introduction

After a long history of failure to reform, American public school systems are undergoing a unique transformation. A grassroots effort, unprecedented in the history of American education, has begun, and is being led, not by education professionals, but by parents. With the advent of educational choice through charter schools, vouchers, virtual schools, and home schooling (which is heavily dependent on online and correspondence courses) as well as traditional public schools, parents are approaching education as consumers. And they are not shying away from school choice. More than ever, they see themselves as having the power to customize their children's education to ensure they receive the best one possible.

Choosing a quality school for your child may be one of the most significant decisions you will make as a parent. Yet, few resources exist for parents interested in school choice. A frame of reference for evaluating potential schools is lacking, and I have written this book to provide parents with the information they need to identify the best possible school for their children. It is for parents, grandparents, guardians – anyone who needs a framework for evaluating a potential educational system for children. Parents who are preparing to send their firstborn off to school or are considering home schooling or who live in a setting where there is school choice will most likely have many questions regarding the most appropriate educational system for their child. This book will answer many of those questions.

How to Choose the Perfect School is the culmination of my experiences in the field of education, both as a professional educator and as a parent. As an educator, I have observed parents as they attempt to navigate the world of school choice. Because my respect for parents and their decision-making skills is so great, and because I am a mother of two school-age children, I can easily sympathize with the challenges they face. After reading this book, a parent with a child at the Moscow Charter School, which I founded in 1997, said she knew intuitively that something was wrong when her children were enrolled in a larger district school; this book helped her put her feelings into words. It also helped her realize what had been wrong with her own education when she was growing up. It is for these parents that I have written this book. It is for the 21st century parent who wants to ensure that their child receives the type of education that will enable them to reach their fullest potential.

It was my personal experiences as a parent that motivated me to write this book. More than a decade after I began investigating school options for my eldest child, there are still few resources available to help parents make informed school choice decision. Parents who care enough about the quality of their child's education to consider school options deserve a practical book that they can use to identify the characteristics of good schools and the variables that contribute to a quality education.

It was my experience as an educator that ultimately led me to take the connection between the new findings in learning research and school curriculum to the next level by starting a private preschool and kindergarten in 1992, and then an elementary charter school in 1998. In 1997, with 25 years' experience at all levels of education from pre-school to university and a parent of two young children, I wrote the charter for the Moscow Charter School, the first charter school in Idaho. I have served as Executive Director of the school since then.

To help parents understand the current state of American public education, in this book, I provide a brief history of traditional education theory and the reforms undertaken in response to the prevalent model. I then identify and describe the various school options that are now available. In addition, I also describe recent research into how the brain learns and show how the findings from this research can be used to make small changes in the existing public school system to significantly improve a child's chances of succeeding as a student and as an adult. I also describe the concept of multiple types of intelligence and suggest ways in which schools can engage learners of all types and ages. To provide parents with a premise for evaluating schools, I ask them to devise their own definition of what it means to be a well-educated individual in the 21st century.

Finally, I describe the characteristics of a successful school: the curricular and physical features, which indicate that a school has been designed with the principles of contemporary educational research and theory in mind. This section of the book is meant to be very practical; it is geared toward busy parents who are approaching school choice as consumers. For this reason, I have included an extremely useful tool, a school "report card," in the appendix. This report card, which offers sample interview questions and summarizes each feature described thoroughly in the book, is a handy checklist that parents can use to keep track of the features they are seeking in their child's educational environment. While some of the variables discussed in this book, such as arts courses, foreign language instruction beginning in kindergarten, flexible curriculum design, and block scheduling, do not exist in many schools, I hope they will become standard features in the schools of the future.

CHAPTER 1:

A Parent/Educator's Perspective on School Choice

As consumers, Americans have come to depend on choice. Walk into any grocery store in the nation to buy a box of cereal, and the number of choices will overwhelm you. Ours is a culture that promotes choice. Ten years ago, however, the notion of choice in the public school arena was almost non-existent. Parents were offered a myriad of choices at the preschool level and again at the college level, but the status quo for public elementary and high schools was a mandate from the local school district dictating which school your child would attend.

Ten years ago the notion of choice in the public school arena was almost non-existent.

Before charter schools and vouchers were approved by individual states a little over a decade ago, only parents who could afford private school had a choice regarding the most appropriate educational program for their child. Yet, even with the advent of school choice, many parents believe their children are not getting the education they deserve. Often, it is only children in private schools or those whose parents have extra income who typically benefit from additional enrichment opportunities in the arts, music and athletics. These extra-curricular activities, however, are important to all children; in fact, current research confirms that they are as significant to the development of intelligence and the learning brain as academics.

Today, we are moving into an era where parents of pre-schoolers can expect to have choices at every level of education.

Today, we are moving into an era where parents of preschoolers can expect to have choices at every level of education.

As an educator, I am thrilled about the prospect of a movement that supports school choice as a mainstream part of the American public school system. As a parent, I regret that this movement did not occur sooner. As an educator, however, I know that educational opportunities still vary significantly across the American landscape. All schools are different due to leadership philosophy, staff, resources, and the demographic characteristics of a specific community population. As a parent, I wish all American parents could take advantage of having several quality choices of schools at each stage of their child's education. Even if you live in an area where you think there are few choices, there are alternatives, namely online courses, correspondence courses, and virtual schools, and today, many parents who are not completely satisfied, supplement their child's education with these options.

A good education gives students choices when they enter adulthood and the professional world. It will continue to serve them as they prepare to change jobs or professions. A proficient learning ability and professional choice are the ultimate gifts that parents can give to their children. These gifts are bestowed through the form of education parents give to their children and other types of enrichment that they provide through daily experiences. Many parents realize this, and it is no longer exceptional for them to supplement their child's education with other options. As one home schooling parent said to me, "The possibilities are endless."

When parents face the daunting task of choosing a school, they will have homework of their own to complete in order to determine whether a school's educational philosophy will meet the needs of their children. Foremost, parents must define what they consider to be the characteristics of an intelligent, educated, and successful individual. As a parent, most likely you are already operating under some definition of academic success. Perhaps it was formulated by the philosophy behind the school your child now attends or perhaps your children are not school age, but you have a vague notion about what kind of education you envision for them. On a conscious level, parents should take the initiative to define success as it relates to their child to provide the foundation for making important decisions about their education.

> **Foremost, parents must define what they consider to be the characteristics of an intelligent, educated, and successful individual.**

All parents define educational success for their children, whether by default or by conscious choice, and each parent defines success differently. For example, some parents believe that a quality education should prepare their child to become a doctor, lawyer, or politician. Others are focused only on income and wealth. Some parents are willing to wait until their child's strengths emerge on their own, being content to raise happy children. In Chapter Four, I will guide you to clarify this important frame of reference and explore the idea of developing your own definition of what it means to be successful. Indeed, your definition will influence every aspect of your choice of schools.

After your definition of success is formulated, you will want to visit schools, gather data, and review promotional material. Parents should spend a minimum of one hour at a potential school interviewing the principal and observing classrooms; the school report card at the end of this book will help them formulate a list of meaningful questions. At the Moscow Charter School, parents often spend as much as a half-day at the school, visiting classes and allowing their children to participate in activities with the class into which they might enter.

I used current research findings in brain-based learning to evaluate schools for my own children. During this process, I noticed that most of the schools I visited were based on a century-old model of education called the factory method. This model focuses primarily on rote learning in an effort to prepare students to perform well on standardized tests. At many of these schools, enrichment courses, such as foreign languages and the arts, were cut due to inadequate state funding. I realized that if I allowed my children to attend this type of school it would be up to me, not the school system, to make the connection between the new learning research findings and educational practices through extracurricular, specially-designed learning activities.

Although my primary goal for writing this book is to help parents identify a school program that will provide the best educational option for their child, a second goal is to assist them in determining whether their current school system is providing the best possible education for their child. Sometimes, a child's behavior, such as loss of self-confidence and reluctance to participate in learning, indicate problems in school. In these situations, the school will often blame the child, and it will be the parent's responsibility to assess the situation and determine whether the problem is academic, social, or both. Parents with children already enrolled in school can learn a lot about a school's philosophy and curriculum simply by observing what type of homework their child brings home.

For decades, both educators and non-educators alike have criticized America's public educational system for having a lack of imagination. Some reformers have suggested that the only way to change the current traditional public education system is to throw out everything and start anew. However, research on how the brain learns suggests that many small changes can be made to improve the quality of the traditional system. In fact, some American schools are now using these findings to create an educational environment that is producing well-educated students. This book will help parents identify those schools that have based their design and teaching techniques on research-based principles of success versus schools that are designed to accommodate the adults working there, not the students.

This book will also assist a new type of parent that has emerged with school choice. These parents are picking and choosing available components of many different public and private programs to design a unique program for their child. For example, some parents enroll their child in two schools at once, while others have their child attend a specific course at a local school while they also are being home-schooled. There are also parents who want their child to take coursework all year around and supplement their child's education with on-line and correspondence courses. It is not uncommon today to have high school students enrolled in their local secondary school and university and take online courses, all at the same time. This book will also be of value to the parent who is designing an educational program for a child who has failed in traditional programs, to parents who seek an alternative to the traditional public school, or those who simply want greater flexibility than the local school system offers.

Concluding Chapters 3, 5, and 6 is a summary of the information parents will need to choose a school or create their own diverse educational experience through a combination of programs. As a result of my experiences as a parent and a professional educator, I have observed many sides of the school system in the United States, and I am committed to trying to improve the quality of education American children

A substantive education includes the ability to identify and to solve real world problems and to generate creative solutions

receive. This is one reason I am an advocate of school choice. One type of school cannot serve the needs of all of America's families and students. A child who shows talent in music should be able to attend a school that emphasizes the arts, not engineering. While I have designed a charter school that offers a high level of enriching activities for both teachers and students, on the other hand, I also have observed that some students perform better in a highly structured environment with little variation in subject matter.

Further, educators now know that there are certain variables that will expand a student's potential for deep learning and thinking that can provide a foundation for success in later life. In my professional career, I have discovered that a substantive education is more than rote memorization of academic material. A substantive education includes the ability to identify and solve real world problems and to generate creative solutions; including problems as complex as supporting the decision to send our nation off to war or as simple as planning a vacation. Real world decision making skills may be more important to a successful adult than learning a large body of specific facts after the basic skills are learned and it is solutions to problems like these that will continue to have a significant impact on the quality of our lives. In fact, only a few professions, such as medicine, require an individual to immediately recall specific facts on a regular basis. The rest of us may rely more on organizational skills, team work, the ability to recognize when there is a problem to be solved and the skills and knowledge of where and when to research related facts needed to reach a solution.

Educational research demonstrates that enriching activities, such as training in the arts, play an important part in preparing a student to meet the types of challenges posed by our complex and rapidly changing society. When schools single-mindedly place an emphasis on teaching only those skills that can be measured on standardized tests, they are sacrificing valuable learning opportunities for students. Based on documented research findings, if education is to be truly effective, enrichment activities should be offered as part of the standard curriculum starting in the early years. A government that takes away the local control of public schools by giving them unfunded mandates that contain rigid rules about testing and standards criteria such as in the federal "No Child Left Behind Act," may inadvertently be creating a public school system that is preventing American students from reaching their fullest potential.

CHAPTER 2:
From Bobbitt to Bush: Has Anything Changed?

The history of the development of American public school curriculum sheds an important light on what is happening in some of our schools today. A curriculum, generally defined as the aggregate of courses offered by a school, also includes the components of school design, course format, class configuration, and student placement within the system. As long as there has been formal public schooling in the U.S., there has been conflict among professional educators over what an effective curriculum should contain. Traditionally, educators fell into two camps.

As long as there has been formal public schooling in the U.S., there has been conflict among professional educators over what an effective curriculum should contain.

One group was more concerned with nature and children, and what they saw as health and wholeness, than with intellectual growth; the other side stressed high academic achievement. As early as 1902, philosopher John Dewey proposed the utopian idea of combining these two educational theories based on his view of education as a dynamic process. Inspired by Ralph Waldo Emerson (who wrote the *American Scholar*) and Henry and John Thoreau (who founded Walden School) Dewey suggested that educators think about a child's educational experiences as something fluid, embryonic, and vital. Experience without concept, Dewey argued, is shallow and stagnant; concepts without immediate connections to experience are inert and useless. Dewey realized many of his ideas in his laboratory school at the University of Chicago from 1896 to 1903. Interestingly, educators today are still divided between those who believe in curricula that focus on teaching students to perform well on standardized tests and those who attempt to teach the "whole" student through experiential learning.

Another Progressive Era educational theorist was John Franklin Bobbitt. In 1918, Bobbitt wrote the first book on American public school curriculum, *The Curriculum*. This landmark book established the nature of the field of curriculum development and set a precedent for all subsequent approaches to curriculum theory throughout the 20th century. The period during and following World War I was marked by significant industrial growth in America, and Bobbitt was greatly influenced by the principles of scientific management that were being used in industry. In his book, he set about to apply them to education. These principles were based on the philosophy that the student was to be treated as raw material to be transformed into a product.

The paradigm proposed by Bobbitt was called the factory model. It emphasized obedience, rote learning of specific facts, orderliness, and respect for authority. His ideas flourished in the following decade, thanks to educator Ralph W. Tyler. Tyler developed a model of public school curriculum planning that clarified and amplified Bobbitt's view and sought to standardize every aspect of education. The notion of administering standardized achievement tests to all public school students stems from this view, as did the concept that public school administrations should develop a bureaucratic set of rules and regulations to ensure that no school deviates from the suggested norm. During the 20th century, curriculum development at all levels of education was based upon this model. In fact, most public educational institutions extended the original model defined by Bobbitt and Tyler while maintaining the underlying top-down man-

The factory method was based on obedience, rote learning, orderliness, and respect for authority.

agement approach dependent upon standardizing curriculum planning, instruction, and testing.

When I was in elementary school in the 1950s, the school I attended was an exact replication of the factory method. The standard curriculum included classes in reading, writing, mathematics, history, and science. Music and art were not a consistent part of the elementary school curriculum. Students were taught how to read using the phonics method. A single classroom teacher was expected to provide instruction in every subject, and in the same manner: through lecture, workbooks, and work sheets. We were expected to master subject matter through memorization and then recite back the memorized information on standardized tests. In those days, when a student entered this sort of environment in kindergarten or first grade, he or she usually stayed with the same class throughout their entire educational career, regardless of their academic skill level or their ability to excel in specific subjects. Educators had little formal knowledge of different learning styles (the sense or senses that a child predominately uses to receive information, such as vision or hearing) that make each child a unique learner. The underlying premise behind curriculum planning during this era was that students should be molded to the curriculum instead of individualizing the curriculum to fit the child, a child-centered approach that is gaining momentum today.

Occasionally, however, honest efforts were made to reform this paradigm. A few educators recognized that the Bobbitt-based system of curriculum development might not be the best system for educating all children, and they tried to make substantive changes in educational practices and the physical environment of the classroom. In the 1930s, physician and educator Maria Montessori developed an independent learning model based on discovery learning. In the 1950s, psychologists and educators proposed instructional theories that suggested an alternative approach to curriculum development. These theories involved thinking, problem-solving, concept formation, and other cognitive processes.

One such theorist was psychologist Jerome S. Bruner, a researcher who displayed substantial interest in the nature and development of cognitive processes and in their potential implications for education. Much of Bruner's writings and research were based upon theories developed by another psychologist, Jean Piaget in the 1930s. Bruner's theories focused on "inquiry training" or the "discovery learning method." Bruner suggested that the traditional focus of curriculum in the public schools excessively stressed factual details. While Bruner's approach has continued to be popular in subsequent educational reform movements, it has never truly gained a foothold in the general public school system, even though many contemporary learning psychologists share Bruner's concern. In *Successful Intelligence*, Professor Robert Sternberg argues that excessive focus on memorization of facts does nothing to promote "successful intelligence" in an individual. In *The Power of Mindful Learning*, psychologist Ellen Langer suggests that all learning should be deliberate or mindful and that rote learning prevents the learner from learning to develop original hypotheses about events and solutions to unique situation encountered in life.

The movement that emphasized learning through discovery and independent problem-solving (as introduced by Dewey at the turn of the 20th century and refined by Montessori, Piaget, and Bruner) served as the foundation for the development of two types of educational alternatives that started in the 1960s and 1970s: magnet schools and pilot schools. Magnet schools offer programs that emphasize a particular curricular emphasis, such as foreign languages or training in the arts. They were originally introduced to facilitate desegregation and are intimately connected to their communities; they offer a wide diversity of approaches to education and were, in fact, the first schools to introduce the idea of curricular autonomy, an early form of educational choice. Many of these schools are located in the nation's largest cities.

Pilot schools, such as those developed in the Boston public school system in 1994, are similar to in-district charters, established by a local school system, instead of an independent chartering group. They are free of union contracts and school committee rules and regulations during the lifetime of their contract. These schools are to be innovative and replicable and should meet student and staff diversity requirements; they are also fiscally autonomous.

Pilot schools and magnet schools were the predecessors to today's charter schools. Through charter schools, educational reformers are attempting to revitalize traditional public education by introducing flexibility, innovation, accountability, and choice to the system. The idea behind the movement is that communities will create independent, but still publicly funded, schools to explore unique educational approaches. In turn, an authorizing agency, such as a state department of education, a local school district or a university, awards a contract (or charter) to a school, which it holds accountable for achieving the goals specified in the school's charter. Traditional public schools can then observe the results of the innovation as demonstrated by student performance in a particular charter school program. The first charter school legislation was passed in Minnesota in 1991. Over a decade later, there are nearly 3,000 charter schools in 40 states, Puerto Rico, and the District of Columbia, with approximately 750,000 students.

> **Through charter schools, educational reformers are attempting to revitalize traditional public education by introducing flexibility, innovation, accountability, and choice to the system.**

Like charter schools, virtual schools offer an alternative to traditional public schools. Virtual schools are private or charter schools that provide students with a home computer and curriculum materials. Students do classroom work independently and are monitored online by a certified teacher. This type of educational environment often appeals to parents who prefer home schooling.

The ultimate tools for school choice are vouchers. In this model, parents receive a voucher that represents the money allotted by the state for each child in the public system. Parents use the voucher to finance their child's education at any school, including religious-based ones. Vouchers are controversial and have been rejected by most state legislators. Some people view vouchers as a potential threat to the traditional public school because they would give parents with children in failing public schools the option to take their tuition vouchers to private schools, thus undermining the financial base of the local public school system.

Parents Hold the Power

As a professional educator, and as a parent faced with school choice, I have asked myself repeatedly if, aside from a few logistical changes, our public schools have sustained any substantive curriculum advances from the rigid academic environment in which I grew up. Has the essence of public school curriculum changed substantially in the past century? In my mind, the answer is "no" in many cases. With the exception of federal and state mandates to provide special education services to students with disabilities, the essence of the curricula and the methods used to deliver them in many of our public schools is not much different from those of over a century ago.

This is despite the fact that our society has undergone dramatic change. The Bobbitt model may have made sense during the Industrial Era, but we are now in the Information Age. American workers need critical thinking and problem-solving skills in the 21st century job market. Ideally, parents will want to select a school that offers a curriculum that teaches the skills they perceive to be those that a 21st century professional will need. In addition, futurists predict that today's students will hold at least 12 different jobs in their lifetime and change careers at least three different times. How does adopting a century old curriculum model based on rote memorization of specific facts prepare our students for a lifetime of change? Shouldn't we teach our students to think critically and creatively? Aren't these the skills that will support them during periods of rapid change?

> **American workers need critical thinking and problem-solving skills in the 21st century job market.**

Furthermore, reforms like charter schools are swimming upstream against a tide of restrictions created by legislators who bend to the lobbying of school reform opponents. Creative and innovative techniques based on research about how the brain learns are being abandoned to accommodate the intense pressure to ensure that students perform well on standardized tests. Under the federal No Child Left Behind Act, passed by Congress in 2002, all public schools are under the thumb of restrictive federal legislation that supports an increased emphasis on standardized testing. Further, because federal regulations are mandated but not properly funded, already financially strapped public schools are forced to use valuable financial resources to learn to comply with new rules and regulations. These mandates often eliminate any in-depth changes in the nation's public schools that might have occurred during the reforms of the 1960s and 1970s. Ultimately, it will be the parent's job as an educational consumer to decide whether they are willing to accept the status quo or identify and support programs that deliver alternative and expanded curricula.

While parents hold the power that will drive the educational reforms of the 21st century, they must use this power wisely. Over the past seven years, I have observed a new type of parent emerge with school choice that I call a "school shopper." School shoppers are parents who put their children in a different school every year because they become disillusioned or dissatisfied with teachers or schools everywhere they go. This dangerous parental practice has adverse consequences for the welfare of students. Although a certain amount of change is good for developing children and youth, their primary need is for consistency. Further, constantly blaming a school for what may be the child's problems, without making any efforts to create or to sustain change, sends a definite message that problems are always someone else's fault.

The purpose of this book is to help parents identify quality schools that will provide a good fit between their goals and their child's needs. I do not suggest that the school parents choose should have a perfect score on the school report card. Parents should prioritize the features that seem the most important and concentrate on them. Issues may occur after a parent has chosen a school. As an educator, I suggest that parents should not expect to be perfectly satisfied with every single feature of a school or every single teacher their child encounters in a school system. After all, learning to cooperate with someone they might not like or with whom they disagree is an important life skill for children to learn. Learning to deal with adversity leads to resiliency, which psychologists maintain is one of the most important skills for a successful life.

CHAPTER 3:
Brain-Based Learning

Perhaps the most significant findings in the field of education to emerge in the later decades of the 20th century was information provided by a variety of professionals, including psychologists, neurologists, and educators, about the physiology of the learning brain. During the 1990s, researchers used sophisticated medical processes, such as magnetic resonance imaging, to increase our understanding of how the brain works. Now it is possible, as never before, to identify and understand learning processes and to apply teaching methodologies and techniques based on the structure and function of the brain. My foremost advice to parents is to choose those schools that offer curricula and teaching methods based on concrete research results about how the brain learns.

Now it is possible, as never before, to identify and understand learning processes and to apply teaching methodologies and techniques based on the structure and function of the brain.

The notion that learning experiences should be designed around our knowledge of the learning brain is relatively new. Public school systems have typically been designed to accommodate the adults working there, not their students. In the worst case, these schools offer the minimum number of school days required by the state, segmented course offerings with little or no integration, and a curriculum that is devoted directly toward learning only the knowledge that will be tested on achievement tests.

Knowledge about how the brain learns can affect the way we teach in a variety of ways. On the practical side, it can help students understand how to maximize their ability to memorize information and to study for a test. For example, research findings have shown that when memorizing a list of words, an individual will have the greatest long and short-term retention of the words at the beginning of the list. I have used this single piece of information to my advantage, and to the advantage of my children, when I help them learn spelling words, a speech, or a violin solo by putting the most difficult part to be learned at the beginning of the practice session. I have found this technique to be far superior to practicing the material in the same chronological order because it seems to avoid the problem of a learner making the same error in the same place each time. In addition, I have advised my son not to study with music in the background unless it is Baroque. Research has demonstrated that Baroque music, in comparison to other types of music, sets up a rhythmic pattern in the brain waves that enhances cognitive functioning and retention.

Like pieces in a puzzle, educational researchers have identified a number of findings about the learning brain with suggestions for changing the way we deliver formal education.

In this chapter, I summarize literature related to the learning brain. Like pieces in a puzzle, educational researchers have identified a number of findings about the learning brain with suggestions for changing the way we deliver formal education. Many of these individual findings, such as the importance of emotional involvement with the knowledge to be learned, are necessary for long-term retention; they are also subtle, but when viewed as an aggregate, they deliver a powerful message about a quality educational environment. A summary of this knowledge, presented at the end of the chapter and again in the report card in the Appendix, will help parents understand when certain programs will be most beneficial to their child and to determine whether the school they are considering uses current research findings on learning to provide a quality learning environment.

I will also examine the importance of early enrichment techniques, such as offering certain material during critical periods of brain development, emotional involvement, and using meaning to enhance learning. Parents will want to use this information, along with a description of the physical and curriculum features that make up a quality learning environment, when evaluating a potential school system.

Over the past 20 years, brain research has provided us with the information we need to provide a quality education for children. We now can identify and prioritize the hard and soft skills that students need to be successful in the Information Age and include them in curriculum designs. Furthermore, a number of variables enhance and accelerate learning, and these variables can easily be incorporated into a traditional system and used to make a personal connection between the material and the student. In the summary and the report card, there are suggested interview questions that will help parents determine whether the following principles drive the curriculum delivery in a particular school:

* Introduces information and concepts during critical periods of learning (Diamond and Hopson, 1999)
* Allow students to learn information through a variety of modalities, or senses (Gardner, 1983, 1993, 1999)
* Understands the importance of early enrichment (Gardner, 1999)
* Combines emotion with the learning experience (Rose, 1987)
* Uses themes to attach meaning to learned material (Rose, 1987)
* Provides emotional security in the learning environment (Rose, 1987)

Ideally, knowledge of how the brain learns should affect how we teach. Educational researchers share the conclusion that certain features must be present in the learning environment for substantive learning to occur. These features include novelty of learned material (the material should capture a student's attention), presenting material to several modalities or senses (teachers should present information using many different types of activities), and integrating information into a meaningful context (the material should be centered around meaningful themes). Creating an educational environment based on general knowledge of how the brain learns can create a streamlined and efficient learning environment that will facilitate and accelerate learning.

Critical Periods of Learning

For optimal learning to occur, the student must be ready to learn. Research findings on the learning brain demonstrate that educators can accelerate and enhance learning by offering enriching opportunities during "periods of readiness" that naturally occur in the development of the human brain. These findings show that in some instances learning appears to happen spontaneously if the learned material is presented during periods when the brain is "ripe" for receiving information. Because critical periods also build upon previous learning, it is important for a student to stay on course with developmental skills if learning opportunities are to be maximized. It is commonly accepted among educators that during a person's lifetime the most receptive period for developing a foundation for emotional, social, and academic learning is between birth and 12 years of age, although the critical period for learning some information, such as emotional maturity, is in infancy or early childhood.

...the most receptive period for developing a foundation for emotional, social, and academic learning is between birth and 12 years of age...

Dramatic examples of the concept of critical periods of readiness for learning can be seen in children who spend infancy in orphanages where care is poor and intimacy lacking. Because the critical period for bonding with others and for the development of emotional intelligence occurs in infancy, children raised in an environment lacking in intimacy are often unable to establish meaningful emotional bonds with others throughout the rest of their lives.

Other examples of this concept are seen in research on bilingual children. Studies have demonstrated that if a child learns a foreign language before the age of seven the brain stores the language learned in the same area as the native language. However, after the age of seven, foreign languages are stored in a different area of the brain. Learning a second language becomes progressively more difficult each year, if the learner is over the age of seven. It is surprising that many school systems begin foreign language instruction in junior high school after this critical period is over.

The Suzuki music instruction method also takes advantage of these "windows of time" by teaching students to play musical instruments at an early age. With this method, before the students even begin to play, parents repeatedly play an audiotape in the background containing the songs to be learned throughout the day. The young student is processing the music during a period of time when the brain is ripe for learning. When this auditory skill, which was developed subliminally, is combined with technical skill developed by the teacher, the ability to play the instrument is multiplied twofold, and rapid progress can be made. It is common knowledge that students trained at an early age in the Suzuki method have strong auditory skills for a variety of subjects, not just music, demonstrating the notion that training in the arts at an early age can enhance all areas of learning and the ability to learn.

Learning to think creatively has an early "critical period" as well. Creative thinking is one of the most important skills that a high-level professional can have, and this skill will promote success in many aspects of a person's life regardless of his or her social standing and formal education. Research has shown that children under the age of five are high in the area of creative thinking and that they use this ability to propel themselves to learn a variety of fundamental motor and verbal skills. Although most individuals start out as creative thinkers, this ability declines rapidly and often begins to be extinguished in the early primary grades. Linear, traditional public school curricula do little to promote creative thinking, and that is the reason it disappears as the child enters grade school. If school systems would devote a certain portion of their

> **Creative thinking is one of the most important skills that a high-level professional can have...**

curricula to supporting and teaching creative thinking skills, such as is done at the well known Italian schools founded by educator Emilio Regio, then individuals would most likely maintain a high level of creative thinking throughout their entire educational career. Early on, Emilio Regio schools introduce the concept of project learning. Students are encouraged to investigate multiple solutions to complete projects and solve problems creatively throughout their entire school career.

Consistently incorporating a wide variety of age-appropriate learning experiences into an early childhood or elementary learning environment builds or strengthens neural connections in the brain and generally enhances learning in all areas. Once activated, connections that were established in the early years may support the use of the brain even into old age. For example, geriatric individuals who suffer a stroke have a greater chance of recovery if they had music training in childhood. Encouraging creativity through the arts and project learning in a school curriculum enables students to build upon their innate ability to think and to learn holistically and maintains a greater potential reserve for recovery should brain damage occur.

> Consistently incorporating a wide variety of age-appropriate learning experiences into an early childhood or elementary learning environment builds or strengthens neural connections in the brain and generally enhances learning in all areas.

Multiple Modalities (Senses)

Brain-based learning research supports the notion that greater understanding and retention occurs when multiple modalities, or senses, including sight, hearing, taste, smell, and touch, are stimulated. A school system that bases its curriculum on brain-based learning would not use the memorization of abstract facts as its primary methodology. Rather, brain-based learning research would support the use of lessons that include both intellectual and motor involvement during the learning experience, such as those in which students physically measure objects to understand the metric system. These findings support multi-faceted lessons that deliver information by appealing to all the senses. For example, during the initial stages of learning multiplication tables, students could be given objects that can be organized into an array that can be counted to discover the total number of objects. At the same time, students would be learning to count in two, threes, fours, etc. The teacher, while exposing students to the concept of arrays, also could encourage them to formulate a number model on paper. Another piece of this many-sided approach might be to incorporate the use of memorization to learn multiplication facts.

Increasingly, teachers are discovering that arts education is a teaching tool that touches many modalities including musical, bodily (dance), logical (music), spatial (visual art), and interpersonal and intrapersonal (theater). We have used this knowledge at the Moscow Charter School to design a curriculum that includes teaching morals, intellectual concepts, and factual information based upon a single academic theme studied over the entire year. Also, a school system that gives equal weight to skills in the arts allows teachers and parents to understand the many types of intelligences that a child may possess and helps them develop an appreciation for children who may not have strength in verbal-linguistic abilities but are strong in the area of bodily-kinesthetic, for example. Educators can also teach students to compensate for their weak areas by presenting information through one or more of their strong areas. For example, a teacher could help a student who is having trouble memorizing multiplication tables by presenting them as a song.

Early Enrichment

In *The Disciplined Mind*, psychologist Howard Gardner lists seven findings based on the physiological development of the brain that he believes are essential information for all educators to know. Four of these findings support the concept of early enrichment as a method for enhancing or accelerating learning. They are:

1) The importance of early enrichment. Although all experiences in life contribute to the learning brain, those that occur in early life during critical periods of learning are particularly important for all individuals. Ideally, an eclectic set of educational experiences should begin early in life in order to produce a diverse learner (Diamond and Hopson, 1999).

2) "Use it or lose it." If neural connections in the brain are not created and stimulated through the senses in the early years and then used actively over a period of time, these connections may eventually atrophy. This finding supports the notion that it is valuable to present a diverse set of learning experiences that reinforces prior knowledge over time.

3) The flexibility of the early nervous system. Research shows that alternative areas of the brain can compensate for those areas injured or damaged, particularly in young children. As we age, however, our brain becomes less flexible and less able to compensate for lost capacities and functions.

4) The organizing role that music plays on the brain. Learning a musical instrument early in life enhances other learning areas, including traditional curricula, such as reading and math. Studies on adults who suffer from aphasia suggest that recovery is more certain and greater in scope if the individual has had training in music as a child. In *Magic Trees of the Mind*, Marian Diamond and Janet Hopson report that studies have also shown that stimulation of a fetus with music and the human voice can accelerate physical and mental developmental stages after the baby is born.

Emotion and Meaning

Brain-based research shows that retention of material is most efficient when learners combine meaning and emotion with the material to be learned. One way for teachers to evoke emotion is through the delivery of information through the use of themes. Teachers who design an entire unit of academic and arts activities, such as a reading, English, and history lesson around the specific theme of "Native American Culture," for example, are using the findings of brain-based research. Emotion can also be evoked by simulating real life situations in the classroom, such as allowing students to set up a store to practice making change or by having a mock trial to learn about history. In addition, researchers have discovered that foreign languages are learned faster when meaningful situations are acted out in the classroom; this is because the phraseology is learned in context.

As an educator and a parent, combining emotion with learning makes sense to me. Because all the skills we need in our personal and professional lives occur in a specific context, teachers should minimize the memorization of abstract material in the classroom and draw upon techniques that simulate real world situations. Boredom and the inability to concentrate occur when learning a task, such as memorizing a list of history dates or spelling words, because novelty is lacking; it is simply too abstract. The brain will retain the information but only in short-term memory. Rote memorization of academic material is only useful if it is preceded by or followed by activities that use the information in a meaningful way.

> **Rote memorization of academic material is only useful if it is preceded by or followed by activities that use the information in a meaningful way.**

Learning Styles

Although brain-based learning techniques generally apply to all students, it must be remembered that, because each student is unique in their development and life experiences, they each have a particular learning style. A learning style refers to the dominant modalities, or senses, that a student uses when processing and remembering information. Some students process and remember information better if it is presented visually (the information is read by the students). Others learn faster through an auditory presentation (lecture), and yet others may learn through tactile, or hands-on, activities. Teachers who support the concept of different learning styles and present a variety of different types of lessons that appeal to all five senses will provide the optimum conditions for learning for an entire classroom of diverse learners. Parents of children with special learning needs should evaluate a school for a flexible curriculum delivery system. Does the school offer specialized instruction for non-traditional learners? Does it have classroom teachers who are willing to try different methods of information delivery? Does it provide additional professionals, such as a special education teacher, a language therapist, or a teacher's aide to be in the classroom during basic skills instruction to assist the student?

Relaxation, Music, Movement

In *Accelerated Learning*, educator Colin Rose examines 25 years of research that has led to the development of techniques that present information to both the unconscious and conscious mind. When academic learning is combined with music, movement, or presented thematically, Rose shows that learning is accelerated and made effortless.

In *Making Connections: Teaching and the Human Brain*, authors Renate Nummela Caine and Geoffrey Caine support Rose's conclusions and suggest that the following techniques also enhance learning:

• *Relaxation*: Rhythmic breathing and creative visualization are essential to effective relaxation, and relaxation is the key to effective learning.

• *Music*: Georgi Lazanov and other researchers have found that music (especially that performed with stringed instruments) from the Baroque period of the early 18th century has a profound effect on learning. The music, which is constructed in 4/4 time with 60 beats per minute, is said to entrain the heartbeat and mental rhythms to affect a physically relaxed yet mentally alert state.

• *Movement*: Inactivity can impair learning. In fact, some students need extensive mobility while learning. These active learners encode information through a whole-body and brain integration experience (Ostrander and Schroeder, 1991). Exercises in cross body movement (e.g. some types of dance or gymnastics-type of exercises) have been found to engage both sides of the brain and have a generalized positive effect on learning. In his book *Teaching With the Brain in Mind*, educator Eric Jenson, reports that there is substantial biological, clinical, and classroom research to support a strong link between physical education and learning and the arts and learning.

• *Peripherals*: Learning is influenced in a positive way by surrounding peripherals such as smells, colors, and sounds

(Jenson, 1994). When educators use decoration, sound, smells, and other stimuli pertaining to the subject matter during a lesson, it has been found that presenting some of the same peripherals later on, can help students recall information that was initially learned.

• *Mentoring*: Instructing others helps the teacher retain the material (Rose, 1987). Allowing students to mentor each other can be an interesting and engaging activity with positive results.

Emotional Security

Research shows that a student must feel safe, unthreatened, and relaxed to achieve significant learning. Children who are stressed from any number of circumstances, such as poor classroom conditions, bullying by other students, lack of attention from parents or teachers, or a poor diet are compromised when it comes to learning. Teachers and schools can maximize feelings of security by practicing consistent and positive classroom management rules and providing a clearly defined schedule throughout the day.

Summary

The growing body of brain-based learning knowledge suggests that educators need to move beyond simplistic, narrow approaches to teaching and learning. Research shows that learning engages the entire physiology, that it is enhanced by challenge and inhibited by threat, that emotions are critical for patterning, and that the brain remembers best when facts and skills are embedded in natural spatial memory. There is strong evidence for moving away from curricula based on linear instruction that is dependent on abstract work sheets. Teachers who incorporate research from brain-based learning research would:

• Use a curricula that provides early enrichment for a variety of hard (basic academic skills) and soft skills (emotional and psychological skills).

• Take into consideration different learning styles, knowing that different learners use different senses when learning. For example, a teacher who relies heavily upon worksheets is not following principles of brain-based learning.

• Design daily lessons that evoke emotion in the learner. Project-based learning, such as acting out a character in a book they are reading, helps students interact with the project, thus triggering emotion during the lesson.

• Know that schools should provide emotional security and a feeling of safety for their students by reinforcing positive social behaviors and providing swift and clear consequences for inappropriate behavior.

• Create a classroom environment and activities that encourage relaxation.

• Use a curricula that includes strong music, arts, and movement programs for students of all ages.

Brain-based Learning: Sample Interview Questions

–Describe the kindergarten curriculum.

–What grade level does the school begin teaching the basic skills of reading, writing, and mathematics?

–What specialized classes does the school offer every student, including those in kindergarten?

–Does the teacher use a variety of ways, including hands-on projects to supplement work sheets and to introduce important reading, writing, and math concepts?

–Does the school or individual teachers use themes to introduce and tie together academic activities?

–What type of support specialists does the school have to assist non-traditional learners or students with learning problems?

–Describe the school and classroom schedule.

–What steps does the administration take to insure that all students will be safe on the school grounds?

–What is the school's philosophy regarding bullying and how does it respond to students who bully other students?

Brain-Based Learning Features	What a School Should Offer:
Critical Periods of Learning	__ Mastery of basic skills: reading, writing, and mathematics in grades K-6. __ Foreign language instruction beginning in kindergarten. __ Arts training, K-12, to nurture and foster creative thinking. __ Activities that promote problem-solving, e.g., hands-on math and science, K-12.
Multiple Modalities (Senses)	__ Variety of courses that use multiple senses, including art, music, physical education, dance, and theater. __ Integrated coursework, e.g., a humanities program including English, history, art, music, and foreign language tied together with a single theme.
Early Enrichment	__ Full range of enrichment courses beginning in kindergarten and extending through high school, e.g., reading, writing, arts, foreign language, physical education.
Emotion and Meaning	__ Daily lessons that include meaningful activities, simulations of real life situations, and themes, e.g., building a model to illustrate a story or a hands-on science projects.
Learning Styles	__ Flexible curriculum delivery for non-traditional learners. For example, if a child is having difficulty learning a subject through lecture and worksheets, the teacher should be willing to try another method of presentation. __ Additional professionals to serve non-traditional learners, such as supplemental reading teachers, Americorp volunteers who act as tutors, teacher's aides, speech pathologists, counselors. __ Teachers who accommodate learning styles by offering lessons that require students to perform a variety of activities for information rehearsal, e.g., student is expected to practice spelling words using a different activity for homework each night.
Relaxation, Music, Movement	__ Regularly scheduled classes in the arts and physical education.
Emotional Security	__ Safe and secure physical environment. __ Teachers who have been well trained in classroom management and can maintain a structured, positive classroom environment. __ Well-organized school and classroom schedules for students throughout the day. __ A school philosophy that minimizes violent behavior.

CHAPTER 4:

Defining Intelligence and Success in the 21st Century

For the past 15 years, since the birth of my first child, I have given a great deal of thought on how to create the best educational environment possible for my children and others. I even put my ideas into action by founding a private preschool and kindergarten, and a charter elementary school. My first steps in creating these schools were to identify the characteristics of a well-educated individual and to define the concept of intelligence. Every parent who faces school choice will need to take these steps, too. In this chapter, I hope to stimulate parents' thinking processes so that they can create their own definitions of intelligence and what it means to be well-educated and successful. By understanding their own perspectives, parents will be better able to identify or create an educational environment that works for them and their child.

By understanding their own perspectives, parents will be better able to identify or create an educational environment that works for them and their child.

To navigate the world of school choice successfully, parents should have a solid notion of what they consider an educated individual to be. With society changing more rapidly than ever before, the definition of what it means to be an educated individual may be truly open for debate. Never before have we had instant access to, or been so dependent upon, technology for many of our professional needs; never before in our society have we been faced with such rapid change. We are well into the Information Age, yet many of our schools continue to rely on a curriculum model developed during the Industrial Age. Many educators still depend on lessons based on drill and practice instead of interactive learning and use curriculum materials that contain predefined problems that leave students out of the most important part of the problem-solving loop: identifying the problem before solving it. Further, strategies and tools for succeeding professionally in the 21st century, and the science of information management, are generally not taught until a student enters college, long after the critical periods for learning are over.

Some educators suggest that the private education system is producing a small elite that will power America's scientific and political establishment. Private schools, they argue, offer enrichment activities, such as training in the arts, foreign languages, and technology, that many public schools have had to cut because of budgetary problems. As a result, many public schools are "training" students rather than "educating" them. The distinction between "educate" and "train" is an important one for parents to make when they are evaluating schools. If students are being "educated," it is implied that they will acquire deep learning, thinking and problem-solving skills, whereas if they are being "trained," they are expected to do no more than memorize specific information to be recalled later. In addition, parents should be aware that many public schools are overwhelmed by state and federal regulations that emphasize student performance on achievement tests. When this pressure is combined with features that cannot be controlled by a district and that don't necessarily support the ability to provide a quality education, such as the case in a large population of low income students needing to play academic catch up, then these schools may not have the time or the financial resources to offer anything other than training in basic core courses.

Although it is the responsibility of modern educators to define further the difference between educating and training, and to assess the impact these different approaches will have on a

> The distinction between "educate" and "train" is an important one for parents to make when they are evaluating schools.

student's future, parents as consumers will drive this change. If one of the main purposes of education is to teach people to think and to become proficient problem solvers, I believe we need to reassess our concept of what it means to be well-educated, as well as our definition of intelligence.

The ancient Greeks had a broader version of what it means to be well-educated than that which currently exists in American schools. Although many aspects of our society are based upon ancient Greek culture, our modern notion of formal schooling is far removed from the original idea of the purpose of education. For the ancient Greeks, an educated individual was one who was developed in every area; an educated person was one who was knowledgeable, courageous, loyal, and physically strong. A well-developed and educated individual maintained a holistic sense of beauty in body, mind, and spirit.

Over time, however, this holistic view of education gave way to one that made a strong distinction between romantic thinking (the arts) and scientific thinking (the sciences). In this model, the romantic mode of thinking is characterized by imaginative, creative, and intuitive thinking, while reason and concrete laws dominate the scientific mode. Although both views of the world are legitimate, modern educational systems have become locked into one of the two camps, with the scientific method being the preferred model. Curriculum theory of the 20th century, with its emphasis on the factory model, is a perfect example of the preference for the scientific mode of thinking.

By not balancing and integrating the two views, educators are missing out on the potential to enhance and to accelerate learning. In *The Disciplined Mind*, psychologist Howard Gardner suggests that educators should focus on three topics that truly educated individuals should understand in full: truth, beauty, and morality. This focus, with its origin in ancient Greece, would be more in line with our values and professional needs. It is true that appreciation of these concepts, which are often considered secondary to the scientific

> By not balancing and integrating the two views, educators are missing out on the potential to enhance and to accelerate learning.

emphasis, would be difficult to measure on a standardized test, yet current research on how the brain learns may bring education full circle by recognizing the value of a holistic view of intelligence, learning, thinking, and memory. Researchers are finding that the brain learns most efficiently when information is presented in context and with emotion. One way to accomplish this is by integrating the arts—with their reliance on imagination, creativity, and intuition—into curricula.

Defining Intelligence

There is a general perception that intelligence is directly correlated with the concept of what it means to be an educated individual because the two terms have similar characteristics, even though it is possible to be intellectually gifted but poorly educated. In reality, intelligence is a complex issue that should be viewed in a broad perspective. Traditionally, intelligence has been measured through a series of tests that evaluated language, math, memory, and reasoning skills. If one is skillful in these areas, he or she is deemed intelligent; people who are athletically or musically gifted, but measure poorly in the areas measured by intelligence tests, however, are said to have a low intelligence quotient.

While some parents and teachers continue to use performance on intelligence tests to determine their expectations for a child's academic ability, others question this approach. One of the leading proponents of a more balanced definition of intelligence is psychologist Howard Gardner. In the 1980s, he began to challenge the traditional notion of intelligence, with its focus on language, mathematical, and reasoning skills. Gardener suggested that there are several types of intelligence: musical, bodily kinesthetic, logical, mathematical, verbal-linguistic, spatial, interpersonal, and intrapersonal and that each individual is a unique blend of strengths and weaknesses in at least five of these areas.

Gardner's theory of multiple intelligences supports the use of a well-rounded curriculum in schools, one that includes many facets of the arts and physical education as educational tools. As a professional educator, I have observed that an added benefit to using this theory as a basis for curriculum planning and delivery is that it provides a curriculum that not only helps parents and students identify areas of intellectual strength but also allows teachers and mentors to acknowledge and support strengths additional to those in the traditionally-recognized disciplines. By doing so, teachers and parents are strengthening the child's self-knowledge about learning, and subsequently, his or her self-esteem. The theory of multiple intelligences also supports a holistic definition of intelligence and the use of enriching coursework to enhance the core curriculum classes. A comprehensive arts program containing visual art, music, movement, and drama, for example, touches every modality described by Gardner.

Parents should bear in mind that good educators do not "typecast" students; good educators have positive beliefs about a student's learning ability. Research demonstrates that even students with disabilities live up to a teacher's high expectations. Because many types of intelligence cannot be tested, it is important for parents to have reasonable expectations for their children, even if they do not score well on intelligence tests. A fulfilling life is still possible, if their strengths are identified, nurtured, and allowed to blossom.

Parents should bear in mind that good educators do not "typecast" students...

Successful Intelligence

Another psychologist, Robert Sternberg, theorizes that intelligence is a balance of knowing when and how to use analytic, creative, and practical abilities. Through a wide variety of life experiences, he explains, individuals can learn to use these abilities in a balanced way. Sternberg suggests that having the ability to use skills appropriately is a function of successful intelligence. He says, "Successful intelligence is not just a cognitive ability – it's in large part a reflective attitude toward life and how one is living it. If successfully intelligent people are not getting the results that they want, they are capable of using their problem-solving abilities to reassess aspects of the problem and respond appropriately."

Based on his research, Sternberg has identified 20 characteristics that define a successful individual. According to Sternberg, successfully intelligent people:

* motivate themselves.
* learn to control their impulses.
* know when to persevere.
* know how to make the most of their abilities.
* translate thought into action.
* have a product orientation.
* complete tasks and follow through.
* are initiators.
* are not afraid to risk failure.
* don't procrastinate.
* accept fair blame.
* reject self-pity.
* are independent.
* seek to surmount personal difficulties.
* focus and concentrate to achieve their goals.
* have the ability to delay gratification.
* have the ability to see the forest through the trees.
* have a reasonable amount of self-confidence and belief in their ability to accomplish their goals.
* spread themselves neither too thin or too thick.
* balance analytical, creative and practical thinking.

Educators make the distinction between hard skills and soft skills. Hard skills include the basics such as mathematics, reading, and writing. Soft skills include emotional and psychological skills, such as self-motivation or the ability to accept failure. It is interesting to note that all of Sternberg's characteristics are soft skills. Sternberg concludes that those who have a high ability to recall facts, or can reason with facts, do not necessarily know how to use them to make a difference in society or in their ability to succeed, whereas individuals with the characteristics of successful intelligence do.

Creative Intelligence

Throughout history, there have been outstanding individuals who embodied creativity, an essential component of successful intelligence: Aristotle, Michelangelo, Leonardo Da Vinci, Eleanor Roosevelt, Thomas Jefferson, and Albert Einstein, to name a few. Sternberg defines creativity as a process that requires the balance and application of the three aspects of intelligence: creative, analytical, and practical. He views creativity as the bridge between analytical intelligence and practical intelligence with the central span of the bridge being creativity. He says,

> "*The person who is high only in creative intelligence may come up with innovative ideas but will not recognize which are good ones. The person who is high only in analytical intelligence may be an excellent critic of other people's ideas but is not likely to generate creative ideas of his or her own. The person who is high only in practical intelligence may be an excellent salesperson but will be as likely to sell ideas (or products) of little or no value as to sell genuinely creative ones.*"

The notion that creativity is the connector to analytical and practical intelligence encourages educators to give creativity equal weight in curriculum development and to develop innovative techniques to teach and nurture creativity. Including creativity as a variable in the evaluation of students might give us unsuspected insight into each student's personality and learning style.

Including creativity as a variable in the evaluation of students might give us unsuspected insight into each student's personality and learning style.

In *Thinking for Change*, John C. Maxwell cites the results of a survey conducted to discover creativity levels at various ages. The results of the survey are interesting. Only 2% of the adults surveyed, age 35 and up, were highly creative. This 2% creativity measurement showed up with each descending age group until the seven-year-old population; 10% of that population was creative. Most telling was the finding that 90% of the five-year-olds were highly creative. From this survey, it can be implied that if training in the arts is started in kindergarten, a child's natural ability to think creatively can be nurtured and refined along with the analytical skills necessary to learn basic skills. By starting enrichment programs in pre-school and kindergarten, the most critical periods for brain development, creative thinking can be preserved and maximized.

Comprehensive and integrated arts programs can also create opportunities for students and staff to think creatively. For example, in the arts environment at the Moscow Charter School, students focus on researching a year-long theme that has both academic and arts components. Students are encouraged to research the theme and write stories, fables, and poems about it during the fall semester. They also have regularly scheduled class time with a professional storyteller who tells stories related to the theme of study and they "act out" concepts related to the theme in a regularly-scheduled theater class. The faculty and students then come up with an outline for a theater program that summarizes what has been learned about the theme. A play is written during the school year and presented to the community before the school year ends. This protocol enables the entire faculty and student body to be involved in the creative process together.

Sometimes, this program also provides an opportunity for the students to develop emotional maturity, a characteristic of successful intelligence. For example, one year at the Moscow Charter School, teachers and students brainstormed a variety of ideas for a theater production theme, but because only some of the ideas were selected for the production, some students were upset because their ideas were not used. This presented the opportunity for teachers to explain that when professionals work together they must choose those ideas that offer the best set of solutions. By teaching creativity through the arts, the Moscow Charter School students are provided an excellent environment for presenting lessons about group problem-solving and developing personal resilience.

Summary

As we begin to understand the direction that society is headed in this century, parents should expect professional educators to create additional criteria that allow for the measurement of success in the professional world, a measurement based on an individual's ability to think practically, analytically, and creatively. Educators can then, by varying the way they present and retrieve information, define curriculum tools that help students achieve these criteria.

A definition of successful intelligence should be integrated into the general definition of intelligence and what it means to be an educated individual in the 21st century. Schools should encourage students to develop the characteristics of successful intelligence and teach students to think more successfully than previous generations were taught by including project learning, the arts, interactive (discovery learning) activities, technology, field trips, and by bringing outside speakers to the school. This means that educators should teach higher order thinking and problem-solving skills; they should encourage students to recognize problems, consider a variety of solutions, and choose a successful solution based on reasoning skills. These skills require left-brain use of logic and organization, along with right brain use of creativity and imagination. If the workforce is indeed changing, curricula should encourage students to think practically, critically, creatively, and analytically in a variety of courses, not just the obvious ones of math and science. Creativity need not be taught outright, but schools should provide opportunities for it to be developed through project learning in which teachers and students collaborate. If we do so, we may find that we will ultimately improve the quality of life for many Americans. Curricula that stress drill and the practice of "canned" material by using only memorization and worksheets are counterproductive because they contribute to the eventual disuse of

> A definition of successful intelligence should be integrated into the general definition of intelligence and what it means to be an educated individual in the 21st century.

characteristics that are associated with success in life, including emotional intelligence, resilience against failure, and the ability to have clear intuition when solving a problem.

A parent's notion of what it means to be well-educated and intelligent is the foundation for their choosing a school. As parents evaluate potential schools, this concept will help them identify the features that contribute to a successful education, one that includes content mastery, as well as training in analytical, practical, and creative thinking, and problem-solving. The concept will also help parents identify features that lead to the development of well-educated individuals as opposed to those who are simply well-trained. With the advent of public charter schools, vouchers and online schools, more parents will seek out those programs that include instruction in these skills as well as academic ones.

CHAPTER 5:
Curriculum Features that Support Learning

A school's educational philosophy is brought to life by the unique means the faculty uses to approach the school's curriculum plan. Most schools have an overall design plan for presenting coursework to the student body. Some curriculum designs may facilitate learning more than others, and it is up to parents to determine which design suits their child. A school that stresses designing curriculum material so that each student is able to use information in a meaningful way should be considered over a school that cannot specify their philosophical foundation and goals. Also, a high school's curriculum should be geared toward promoting successful intelligence skills in each student. This can be done by offering service learning and school-to-work programs and assisting students in setting professional goals as they progress through the system through easily accessible career counseling.

A school that stresses designing curriculum material so that each student is able to use information in a meaningful way should be considered over a school that cannot specify their philosophical foundation and goals.

Parents should also look for schools that have incorporated brain-based knowledge into their curriculum design. I have come to realize that the ability to memorize is an important skill, especially for students in the early primary grades when they are learning basic skills. Teachers who design lessons that take advantage of knowledge about the learning brain can assist students in developing a solid foundation for memorization skills more efficiently than those who send students home with lists to memorize. An example of this methodology involves the practice of teaching students a list of spelling words each week; this important task can be made easier if the student is asked to use the words in a different meaningful context, such as crossword puzzles or by writing an essay using the words, each day of the week.

Learning, or maintaining, the ability to think creatively and critically and to define and to solve problems are important skills for children to learn. Their natural ability to develop these intellectual constructs should be fostered in the early primary grades through project learning so that their attitudes toward learning are not restricted as they progress through the school system. Traditional educational curricula can discourage the further development of these behaviors because they completely focus on activities that require memorization or continuous rote drill of information presented outside a meaningful context, such as occurs on many worksheets. Thus, often in a traditional education environment, what was once innate behavior in all children that could have been expanded upon with proper fostering, is left to atrophy through the predominant use of instructional practices that require rote, left brain learning of information that is soon forgotten.

Because many of us experienced this type of educational atmosphere as children, we understand the negative consequences of these poor educational practices. Our own experiences as students can provide us with the inspiration to choose a more effective education program for our children. Yet, with the federal No Child Left Behind Act, it is getting more and more difficult for public schools to apply non-traditional instructional practices. The No Child Left Behind Act mandates that all public schools throughout the United States are to define and provide a standardized curriculum in the core subjects of English, mathe-

> Our own experiences as students can provide us with the inspiration to choose a more effective education program for our children.

matics, language arts, and writing for every grade. The content of these subjects must be taught to all students. Mastery of the content is measured on standardized tests on which students must perform well in order to progress to the next grade level. When choosing a school for their children, parents must take a stand on the critical issue of schools that emphasize rote learning and memorization of the skills to be tested as their entire curriculum and those that offer a varied presentation of other types of academic material along with the core courses.

Laying the Foundation with Early Enrichment

In the previous chapter, I discussed the importance of early enrichment, such as classes in the arts, physical education, foreign language instruction, and computer programming, in the context of creating a teaching environment that maximizes learning potential for the brain. From birth through five years of age, children use discovery learning and creativity to learn a tremendous amount of intellectual, social, and motor information. At no other time in their lives do they learn such a varied and large number of skills and information in such a short period of time. As a parent, it is wise to keep in mind that the experiences learned early in life will continue to have a significant impact on an individual through adulthood. A school should take advantage of this information by offering age appropriate exposure to foreign language, art, and music as well as basic math and reading skills as early as kindergarten. Activities that foster an individual's natural ability to think creatively and to learn through discovery should also occur early in specifically designed lessons or in the overall design of the classroom learning environment, also starting in kindergarten.

Basic Skills and Standards-based Coursework

In the past ten years, most state departments of education have become more stringent about having a uniform set of standards for the basic skills that students must learn at each grade level. The terms "standards-based coursework" or "core knowledge curriculum" are often used to describe this approach to curriculum delivery. This approach improved some schools that did not have a well thought out uniform curriculum for basic skills that progresses from one grade to the next to define what students should know at each grade level. With the passage of the No Child Left Behind Act, schools that fail to provide this type of curriculum, or schools with a majority of students who are unable to demonstrate mastery of the required standards at each grade, will be in danger of having their faculty replaced or losing many of their students to other schools.

Acquiring basic skills in reading, writing, and math at each grade level is important for continued academic success for most students. Having a successful academic career will enhance a student's self esteem; however, poor scores on standardized test can have pitfalls as well. Parents should review a school's policy on standardized tests. While these scores can be used to help a parent determine whether their child is experiencing success or failure in learning basic skills, parents should be aware that sometimes they do not accurately reflect a child's true abilities, especially if their child has dyslexia, is an inexperienced test taker, is having a bad day, or has a phobia of taking tests. The practice of using only standardized test scores as a base for all academic decisions about individual students could have a detrimental effect on some of the students.

> The practice of using only standardized test scores as a base for all academic decisions about individual students could have a detrimental effect on some of the students.

Mindful Learning

During the Industrial Era, a premium was placed on rote learning. In fact, almost all K-12 public and private school systems in America were based on rote learning, with the exception of a few unique educational programs that I have mentioned previously, such as Montessori schools and the experimental pilot and magnet schools in the 1970s. Increasingly, learning psychologists and educators realize that in the Information Age rote learning has inherent dangers, especially for American workers. The opposite of rote learning is mindful learning.

In *The Power of Mindful Learning*, psychologist Ellen Langer writes that all skill should be learned "mindfully." She defines learning information mindfully as a process in which individuals remain open to ways in which information may **The opposite of rote learning is mindful learning.** differ in various situations. I believe that the ability to be aware of subtle changes in your life's circumstances and be in control of your response to them, which is the result of mindful learning, may be one of the most important features of successful intelligence.

Langer warns that over-learning the basic core skills in school through repeated memorization works against the use of information in a mindful way. She has proven through a variety of research studies that over-learning information can prevent an individual from creating new solutions to problems. One of the examples Langer uses in *The Power of Mindful Learning* to illustrate this notion of a lack of awareness of more than one perspective, is the practice of teaching Americans to drive in cars that have the control panels on the left side. Individuals who have over-learned the skill of driving a car with controls on the left side may have difficulty driving in Europe in cars where the controls are on the right side. Having over-learned this skill, some individuals may never be able to learn to drive safely in a foreign country where driving standards are the opposite of what they learned originally.

Langer suggests that our educational curricula should have a mindful approach to teaching even the most mundane tasks. According to Langer, this includes always teaching students the continuous creation of new categories, openness to new information, and an implicit awareness of more than one perspective. Many of Langer's research findings identify methodology teachers can use, with only minor changes to their traditional delivery system, to introduce every skill in a way that will enable students to learn it "mindfully." Sometimes, presenting the students with ways to learn mindfully is as simple as rewording the directions students must follow on a particular task. For example, one of Langer's studies demonstrates that retention of reading material is higher if the teacher, when first assigning the book, asks students to identify themselves with its main character, as opposed to just assigning a book for a student to read.

Langer's research also has some important things to say about the perception of how students pay attention. The common notion is that students cannot pay attention unless they are sitting quietly with their eyes on the task at hand. In a research study in which Langer queried teachers and students about paying attention, she discovered that both teachers and students viewed paying attention as attending to non-moving stimuli, which is, in fact, impossible. In reality, paying attention means observing novel, changing stimuli. Langer's research demonstrates that it is natural for the mind to seek variety, and the greater the variety in the learning environment, the higher the interest. Attempting to maintain a student's attention by requiring them to hold an image still is extremely fatiguing. The most effective way to increase a student's ability to pay attention is to train the mind to look for novelty within the stimulus situation through instruction and directions. Teachers should be aware that novelty has to be in the mind of the observer for attention to occur, and attention has to occur for learning to happen.

Daily rote drills and information presented in an abstract manner actually decreases novelty in the learning environment, especially for young children.

Daily rote drills and information presented in an abstract manner actually decreases novelty in the learning environment, especially for young children. It is interesting to speculate that the overuse of traditional curricula based on a series of workbook activities without meaningful follow-up activities may actually hinder the student from learning effectively. In contrast, a well-rounded curriculum with an emphasis on creativity offers the perfect avenue for mindful learning.

It has been my experience as a professional educator that university training programs for educators do not always include an emphasis on these complex notions of mindful learning, attention, and successful intelligence. However, this approach to teaching can often be observed in "natural born" teachers who seem to have discovered it on their own. A teacher who believes in teaching students to evaluate each situation as an independent learning situation prepares lessons that are engaging, challenging, and insightful.

Parents should look for these additional curriculum features:

Thematic Presentation of Curriculum Material and Integrated Courses

Using a meaningful context to teach academic material facilitates learning for students of all age levels. Typically, both elementary and secondary schools offer a variety of independent courses for English, science, and social studies, taught as separate disciplines. Separate, non-integrated courses are contradictory to what we know about brain-based learning because they do not provide conditions for optimal learning.

Through the use of integration and themes, it is possible to provide a meaningful context for learning basic skills that corresponds to state standards for each grade. A meaningful context can be achieved by integrating core courses into a humanities program that includes art, music, history, English, and foreign languages, or even combining courses that include physics and art, for example. This feature is an important part of the curriculum of the Moscow Charter School, where the entire student body studies one theme throughout the school year. Themes that can be adapted for study in all academic and arts courses are chosen by the teachers, and at the end of the year, an original theater production, written by students and staff to demonstrate what has been learned about the theme, is presented.

Problem-solving and Logic Instruction

The ability to formulate strategies and to solve problems are two of the most important skills that any adult will use in the real world. Courses and lessons that nurture and teach logic and

The ability to formulate strategies and to solve problems are two of the most important skills that any adult will use in the real world.

problem-solving should be incorporated into every level of education from pre-school through high school to keep a child's natural abilities in these areas strong. Because these skills are so useful, all students should learn them before they graduate from high school. According to psychologist Robert Sternberg, problem-solving involves a cycle that includes the following six steps: problem recognition, problem definition, formulating a strategy for problem-solving, representing information, allocating resources, and monitoring and evaluation.

Teachers give students a lot of problems to solve, but they rarely teach them how to identify when a problem exists. Surmising that a problem exists may be the most important step toward solving it. Many pre-designed curriculum workbooks define the problem for the student and only ask them to complete step three through six of Sternberg's problem-solving process. Real world problems can be subtle and complex, and teachers should teach students how to recognize the characteristics of a problem situation before it is too late to solve it.

According to Sternberg, a successful person recognizes a problem well before it becomes too complicated to solve and immediately begins the process of solving it after formulating a strategy. Defining a problem once it is recognized will save time in solving it. Also, an individual can recognize that a problem exists but fail to define the problem correctly, which can lead to a solution that never really solves the problem. Sternberg says that because successful people are able to define problems correctly, they solve real problems, rather than extraneous ones. These individuals also know which problems are worth solving and which ones are not.

Strategic thinking is a key component in the ability of successful persons to solve problems. Sternberg explains that successful individuals typically practice long-term strategic thinking as opposed to using quick solutions to problems. Once a strategy is formulated, successful individuals are fairly accurate in representing the situation realistically, while avoiding emotional labels and feelings that can cloud their ability to manage a specific problem. Once a long-term strategic plan is formulated, successful people think carefully about allocating resources for both the short and long-term, and they choose the allocations that will maximize their returns. Finally, a successful person continues to monitor their plan for solving a problem and will make changes if it is not working.

While these characteristics of successful problem-solving are rarely formally taught at any level of public education, courses in philosophy (logic) and computer programming may be helpful in assisting a student to recognize and identify problems to be solved and to analyze multiple solutions while they are solving it. When interviewing a particular school, parents should seek out its philosophy on teaching problem-solving by asking administrators to provide examples of courses that teach problem-solving and logical thinking. Project-based learning, especially when the child has input into the topic, is also an ideal format for helping students learn to recognize and solve problems that occur in the real world.

Arts Instruction

The arts are a vital component of education as demonstrated by multiple studies, which show that arts education impacts student behavior in positive ways. This positive effect is apparent across socio-economic groups with respect to both academic and personal success. When initiated in the early years (pre-school and kindergarten), training in the arts doubles the power of the teaching tool.

The arts are a vital component of education as demonstrated by multiple studies, which show that arts education impacts student behavior in positive ways.

A 2002 National Center for Education Statistics summary report describes the positive outcomes of 14 different arts education programs in public elementary and secondary schools and programs for at-risk youths. These 14 programs served both middle-income public school students, as well as low income students in challenging neighborhood environments, students with disabilities, school dropouts, homeless youth, juvenile offenders, and incarcerated youth. Although these arts programs vary in scope, they all have one thing in common: consistent student exposure to art, music, dance, and theater in order to promote the expression of knowledge and emotion. Some of the positive outcomes resulting from these programs include increased academic success, lower incidence of crime, and greater self-esteem.

Other outcomes of these programs demonstrate that training in the arts builds important workforce skills and higher order thinking skills, such as problem-solving, learning strategies, creative and innovative thinking, and decision-making, according to a 2001 report from the Progressive Policy Institute.

In general, it has been demonstrated that children who study the arts learn to visualize goals and outcomes, show adaptability to change, and are more likely to attend college. A 1999 study conducted by the President's Committee on the Arts and Humanities and the Arts Education Partnership on 91 school districts across the nation found that the arts contribute significantly to the creation of flexible and adaptable knowledge, which workers need to compete in today's economy.

In general, it has been demonstrated that children who study the arts learn to visualize goals and outcomes, show adaptability to change, and are more likely to attend college.

Arts courses encompass several modalities (spatial, kinesthetic, verbal, inter and intra personal, and musical) and when they are used as vehicles for learning and the expression of learned material, the subjects come to life for several different types of learners. An arts program that teaches conceptual and factual information can easily facilitate the creation of new solutions. Arts programming at the Moscow Charter School, for example, offers a variety of opportunities for students to experience working in groups. In art and dance class, individuals use drawing, painting, sculpture, and movement to illustrate an expression of a concept. Students studying the planet Mars, for example, might be asked in dance class to create movements that illustrate a Martian windstorm. The movements generated by the students can then be used in a final choreography developed by the instructor.

Participating in the arts creates an emotional experience that transcends the logical presentation of information because artistic expression is based on the emotional interaction and involvement between the subject and the topic. Training in the arts as part of an additional enrichment program to the core subjects can be a powerful tool for creating an effective learning environment.

Participating in the arts creates an emotional experience that transcends the logical presentation of information because artistic expression is based on the emotional interaction and involvement between the subject and the topic.

Young children naturally think creatively, and schools that fail to offer a diverse curriculum that includes the arts, beginning in the early pre-school and kindergarten years, are losing valuable "windows" of learning time for their students. Schools that fail to offer diverse learning experiences before the age of 12 are producing students with a narrow view of the world. In contrast, students who grow up with training in the arts not only have more diversity in thinking but also are more likely to be creative in their lives and expression.

Through an integrated arts and academic curriculum, students are encouraged to develop minds that can comprehend complex concepts. They gain experience reaching a group goal, and they learn to use compassion in dealing with one another. Finally, students are encouraged to take responsibility for their actions and risk failure. Training in the arts leads individual students to develop well-rounded learning styles and to gain self-knowledge of specific learning strengths. In addition, it teaches and encourages creative thinking and problem solving, necessary skills for 21st century success.

Unfortunately, programs in the arts are often the first to be cut in public schools, especially in poorly funded, rural schools. Those individuals responsible for the cuts are operating under the mistaken premise that students will demonstrate a higher competency in basic skills and perform better on mandated, standardized tests when a greater portion of the school day is devoted to such instruction. They fail to realize that the arts can be used to reinforce knowledge in a mindful way. Research indicates that training in the arts promotes behaviors that are equally as important as basic skills knowledge for future success in the workplace. Integrated arts curricula are flexible, low cost, easy to replicate, and if designed properly can support and enhance the learning of core academic subjects.

Technology as a Teaching and Learning Tool

Teaching students to use technology as a tool for communication, thinking, or problem-solving depends less on the type of equipment that a school has and more on how it is used.

Parents should evaluate a school's overall technology plan when choosing a school for their child. The plan should include both the hardware setup and the school's philosophy for teaching technology. Technology is an important tool in the general intellectual development of children that, if used properly, can encourage and teach successful intelligence skills. It can also be a thinking/learning tool, a vehicle for creative expression, and a tool that will help students solve a variety of problems. Teaching students to use technology as a tool for communication, thinking, or problem-solving depends less on the type of equipment that a school has and more on how it is used. With this view, the student is seen as a programmer and uses technology much in the same way he/she uses a pencil. The teacher is also a programmer when he or she uses technology to support project-based learning. A technology program should emphasize both the preservation of individualized, self-paced learning, as well as opportunities for group collaboration. I believe these goals represent the future in technology education.

Parents should ask to see the mission of the technology program of each school they evaluate. The mission of the Moscow Charter School technology program may serve as a starting point for parents; our mission is to use technology to enhance the intellectual development of each student, to prepare students to live and to work in an increasingly technological society, and to use technology as a tool to improve education delivery. In other words, the overall goal of our technology program is to use all forms of technology as tools to enhance and to extend education beyond the traditional classroom and library.

Children develop attitudes about technology use as early as preschool. Thus, elementary schools are now responsible for shaping the primary attitudes of both children and parents in the effective use of computers and other electronic technology. It is important to teach children that computers are not devices that only entertain.

The use of technology in the classroom should be based on a teacher's knowledge of learning theory. Seymour Papert, the author of LOGO, a programming language for children, as well as several books about children and technology, has heavily influenced the Moscow Charter School's philosophy, which states:

* technology use should be based on knowledge of learning and brain development.
* technology is an ideal tool for expression, thinking, and problem-solving.
* intensive use of technology will change a child's thinking style and brain development; therefore, technology use in the classroom should be well thought out by the teacher.
* technology should be used to teach children to think in better ways.
* technological opportunities should be turned into learning advantages.
* technology should not be used to "sedate" young children.
* technology can be used to enable a child to find his/her personal path to learning or their own natural learning style.
* the role of the technology teacher is to create conditions for the invention of knowledge.

One of the long-term goals of every teacher should be to encourage students to develop successful intelligence as well as to teach them to think more successfully than previous generations. Higher order thinking and problem-solving, as skills that require left brain use of logic and organization along with right brain use of creativity and imagination, can be nurtured if technology is used in the proper way.

The ideal school has adequate computer-to-student ratios in every classroom and uses a project-based model that emphasizes problem-solving and critical thinking with technology as a tool. With this approach, students and faculty come to understand the possibilities that technology can offer to enhance thinking skills and to take projects beyond the limits of the traditional classroom. A self-paced program that presents information to students in an integrated format that facilitates discovery and emotional involvement during the learning process, which, in turn, enhances meaning and retention for the learner, is to be sought. For example, all third through sixth grade students at the Moscow Charter School are taught computer programming as a method to improve their problem-solving skills. At the end of the school year, students are required to write a software program that will teach other students something, such as teaching kindergarten students to learn shapes or alphabet letters. During the final phase of the project, the programmers test their designed programs on the younger students to better understand the effectiveness of their idea. Other uses for technology in the classroom are to create a self-paced learning environment, integrated thematic instruction, and foreign language instruction. Students should also learn World Wide Web searching techniques in order to expand their ability to conduct research about a topic; they should also be taught the rules of Internet safety. Word processing applications encourage students to write highly polished essays and research papers because of their unique editing capabilities. Technology-based multimedia productions provide a useful adjunct to talks and presentations.

> Teaching our students to realize that most real life problems are not solved neatly and that there are a variety of solutions to almost every problem can be achieved by teaching students to think like programmers.

Learning a programming language or learning to program a computer application further reinforces a student's ability to learn other languages. It also provides a rich environment in which students learn to approach a variety of problems with a variety of solutions.

Teaching our students to realize that most real life problems are not solved neatly and that there are a variety of solutions to almost every problem can be achieved by teaching students to think like programmers. An excellent example of the application of this concept occurs at the Moscow Charter School when students write an original computer program. The students' programs are usually different from one another, and they almost never get the intended outcome right the first time. An overall curriculum that encourages the principle that "if at first you don't succeed, try again" fosters a thinking style that approaches problems without fear and with an attitude that is open to finding multiple solutions. Learning to use creativity in one's approach to finding solutions will ultimately contribute to the future success of the individual. These are important learning opportunities every school should provide.

Another example of the natural integration of technology training into students' overall learning experience is our school-wide money system. This system teaches students three basic concepts: wage-earning, money management, and the use of technology to manage money efficiently. The participants in the program are students in grades three through six.

Each year, the Moscow Charter School prints its own currency in denominations of one, five, ten, twenty, and one hundred. Teachers regulate the distribution of money according to their own classroom plan. Generally, students earn wages by performing jobs within their classroom. The system also provides an opportunity for students to spend the money they earn. Each month, a different classroom prepares a market at which items created by the students in that classroom are sold to the entire school. The theme of the market is usually related to the year-long theme that is being studied throughout the school. For example, one year the overall theme was cultures around the world; therefore, each class used a separate culture, such as Spanish or Egyptian, as the theme of its market. In preparation for the market, students studied the goods of that particular culture and created handmade products to sell on market day. All students were free to use their school money to buy products sold at the market.

One of the first things students do in the system is to establish a bank within their classroom where cash and statements are stored. Each month, a different student is appointed to be the banker. The other students open accounts in the bank and maintain both handwritten ledgers and electronic spreadsheets to track their financial transactions. Students keep a running balance of their accounts and learn to use a checkbook, to read bank statements, and to use electronic spreadsheets to verify handwritten ledgers. Registers maintained as spreadsheets are updated at the beginning of each month, immediately after payday and the day the market is held. Students print out their spreadsheet bank statement and reconcile their checkbooks against the statement. Through this program, we have found that students make a variety of important discoveries about money management and entrepreneurship. Research in brain-based learning supports project-based tasks that enable students to learn within context and to drive the pace of their own learning through the use of simulations, visualizations, and interactive software.

> **Technology facilitates student-to-student teaching and mentoring...**

As a technology teacher, I have observed another benefit of using technology as a teaching and learning tool. Technology facilitates student-to-student teaching and mentoring because it provides an environment that lends itself to these activities. Students who grasp technology concepts faster than other students can be encouraged to become "teachers" and teacher helpers for other students. In addition, technology encourages students to complete projects as a group, with individuals assisting each other in achieving the intended outcomes. Research on learning confirms that the greatest retention occurs when students mentor each other.

Physical Education, Movement, and Dance

In his book, *Teaching with the Brain in Mind*, Eric Jenson states that there is substantial biological, clinical, and classroom research to support the notion that the areas of the brain affected by physical education, movement, and games are linked to the cognitive functions of memory, spatial perception, language, attention, emotion, and nonverbal cues. Yet, studies show that a majority of K-12 American students do not participate in daily physical education programs. Contrast this with additional evidence showing that, not only does exercise fuel the brain with oxygen, it also feeds it neurotropins (high-nutrient food) that enhance growth and greater connections between neurons. Additional research reveals that students engaged in daily physical education show superior motor fitness, academic performance, and a better attitude toward school than students who do not exercise. Jenson also cites research confirming that adding a strong arts curriculum, including dance, provides a creative core that enhances academic excellence.

School-to-Work Programs

Many high school students are uncertain about their futures. High schools with programs that provide opportunities for students to work for local businesses allow students to pursue areas they may be interested in for future careers and help smooth their way into the workforce. Additionally, experience in the community helps students gain experience in making meaningful career choices. To assist students learning more about the working world, some innovative high schools have a curriculum framework that treats every student as a professional. In these schools, students can view their role as an employee in a business, and they are expected to dress and act as professionals.

Communication and Goal Setting

Administrators and teachers should make it a priority to devote time to meet with parents to set goals for the student and solve problems regarding student placement and academic and behavioral failures, and to acknowledge and encourage successes. A school should have an overall defined strategy for setting student goals, such as having parent conferences twice a year, and a feedback mechanism for parents who wish to be involved in the goal setting process. For example, at the Moscow Charter School, parents have the option to fill out a form at the beginning of the year that indicates their yearly academic goals for their child and to schedule a conference with their child's teachers to discuss these goals.

Service Learning

Parents who feel that learning to "give back" to the community is an important step in personality and character development should look for a service learning component in a school's curriculum. Some schools, especially high schools, have specifically designed courses that allow a student to perform a needed service in a community. This type of program gives students realistic experience in understanding and solving problems that may occur in the real world.

Standardized Testing

With the passage of the No Child Left Behind Act, all American public schools are required to use standardized tests to evaluate their students' progress on the basic skills of reading, writing, and math. Until recently, many schools used the Iowa Test for Basic Skills to evaluate student achievement for select grades. These tests, which were conducted once a year, produced a single student score in the areas of reading, writing, and math and were contrasted against a national norm score for each grade and subject. Some educators touted these scores as a sign that their school was academically superior and based many decisions about a student's intelligence and academic achievement on them.

However, many educators felt that this score was vague and hard for parents to understand, especially when their child was compared to every other student in the nation at the same grade and subject. Educators also felt that these scores did not really measure whether a student had made progress in a particular area because they referred more to the student's test taking ability in comparison to other students. Often, schools that felt this way about the tests kept them on file to meet state regulations but never reported them to parents because they believed that the scores had no real significance; all they did was either confuse parents or trigger anxiety that their child was performing below the national norm which, in turn, interfered with their positive expectations.

Since enactment of the No Child Left Behind Act, however, a new type of achievement test has gained popularity. This type of test measures student achievement from the beginning of the year to the end in each of the basic skills areas. Progress is measured individually. This achievement score is helpful to parents and teachers because it measures achievement for a particular year. The test also produces a single percentage score for each classroom that can be used to determine how many students reach the goal of learning the information they are required to learn in a particular grade. In addition, administrators can use this score to determine how effective a particular teacher is in teaching basic skills.

A firm foundation in basic skills and analytical thinking is necessary to achieve some types of professional success. Also, standardized testing is an important accountability tool for schools. However, the current practice of using standardized test scores (which generally measure only the retention of factual information and analytical skills) as the only tool for making sweeping generalizations about the success of a student or a school needs to be reexamined.

Analytical skills, while good predictors of school success, are not necessarily related to success in other environments. An environment that focuses on teaching to the test, with its emphasis on developing analytical skills, includes greater periods of time spent on the linear presentation of basic skills. Educators caught up in this conflict often feel that longer school days and repeated delivery of factual information in a linear way (and sometimes cheating on test results!) are the only responses to the political and professional pressure

The kinds of characteristics that define successful people are impossible to measure on standardized tests.

to get students to perform well on these standardized tests and schools to look like they are performing well.

The fallacy of using standardized test scores as the only predictor of successful academic performance is supported by Daniel Goleman in *Emotional Intelligence* and Howard Gardner in *Frames of Mind*. Goleman and Gardner suggest that successful individuals, who may or may not succeed on conventional tests, are, more importantly, able to capitalize on their strengths and compensate for their weaknesses. Also, according to Sternberg, successfully intelligent people defy negative expectations. They realize that surmounting obstacles is part of the challenge in achieving their goals. The kinds of characteristics that define successful people are impossible to measure on standardized tests. By presenting students who perform poorly on standardized tests with the data that they are "below normal," the formal education system is labeling the student as being impaired, presenting an avoidable obstacle to overcome on their journey to becoming successful individuals.

Parents should acknowledge that professional success is significantly related to a set of psychological behaviors and that it is equally important to nurture them in a school setting. All types of student behavior should be viewed as modifiable. Schools that emphasize rote memorization and linear presentation of abstract facts are presenting information in an inefficient and difficult way for students to assimilate and are also failing to take advantage of critical periods of learning.

Parents should ask school administrators about their achievement testing policies, including what types of tests are used and how the schools use the data from both individual scores and group scores. Most importantly, parents will want to know whether the test score is used to improve their child's performance or if it lowers the expectations of the teachers. Furthermore, parents should always remember that a poor test score does not necessarily indicate that their child will not be a successful adult.

Summary

The notion of mindful learning is subtle but powerful, with significant consequences for life in the 21st century. Technology has led to an information explosion, and it would be impossible to memorize all the information relevant to a particular profession. Practically speaking, for most professions there is no reason to rely totally on memorization now that we have access to technology that can provide reference material in an instant. As we move away from the paradigm of memorizing information, information management becomes a very important career skill. The concept of mindful learning also leads us to question if public school curriculum content has changed over the past century to accommodate real world circumstances.

Including the arts and technology in a school's curriculum gives students many opportunities to learn soft skills and to develop good problem-solving abilities. By analyzing the skills that are taught through arts education, educators have discovered that such training actually enhances intellectual development and accelerates learning ability on all levels. Educational research repeatedly demonstrates that training in the arts makes students creatively and educationally diverse, which enhances the development of skills that will help them function more successfully. Consistent and broad training in the arts throughout early childhood, with an emphasis on creativity, also enables students to become more efficient learners, thus reducing the amount of time they need for drill and practice.

Based on our experiences with an integrated art, music, dance, and theater program at the Moscow Charter School, we have observed that allowing students to participate in the creative process through a comprehensive arts curriculum further enhances student learning and outcomes in many unsuspected areas. These include continued refinement in the area of problem-solving, the discipline of taking an idea from the beginning through to the end, discovery of new talents and abilities, and increased self-esteem. In addition, by working cooperatively and equally with students, teachers are often more creative themselves. Additional benefits include:

- Curricula that uses art as a tool for teaching creative, analytical, and practical intelligence
- The opportunity to experience the balancing of other types of intelligence with analytical skills
- The experience of teachers and students creating works together
- Personal growth for both faculty and students
- Students realizing the importance of working together to solve problems that are both hypothetical (fantasy) and real (factual)
- The opportunity for students to seek answers on their own
- The opportunity for students to develop a well-rounded learning style and gain knowledge of their specific learning strengths
- Reinforcement of mindful learning in a variety of subjects and contexts

Curriculum Features that Support Learning: Sample Interview Questions

- How Does the No Child Left Behind Act affect the school's curriculum?
- Have courses been cut from the curriculum as a result of this legislation?
- Does the school offer a humanities program?
- Are basic skills courses offered every day at the elementary level? What time of the day are they offered?
- Is the content of the basic skills courses based on state standards?
- Is the school curriculum aligned – is it required that content flow from one grade to the other?
- How does the school use thematic learning?
- What types of specialized classes does the school offer besides basic skills courses?
- Does the curriculum include regularly-scheduled physical education classes?
- What is the school's philosophy on teaching the arts?
- What is the school's philosophy on teaching technology?
- What types of activities are included in the technology curriculum at each grade?
- What are the school's and teachers' systems for classroom management?
- Does the school offer parent/teacher conferences? How often?
- How often are report cards or progress reports sent out?
- Does the school encourage parent volunteers?
- Do administrators and teachers use test results from standardized tests to improve instruction for each student?
- Does the school offer school-to-work programs?
- What type of career counseling is available at the school?
- Does the school offer service learning programs?

Curriculum Features	What a School Should Offer:
Early Enrichment	__Curriculum that emphasizes early enrichment by offering specialty classes beginning in kindergarten. __Classes in basic skills, arts, and foreign languages starting in kindergarten.
Basic Skills: Reading, Writing and Math General courses	__Basic skills coursework for each grade that is based on state or national standards. __Mastery of basic skills for students in K-6, with these courses scheduled in the morning. __Curriculum in which social studies and science are offered as standard courses in all grades starting in kindergarten. __Standardized test scores for each teacher showing that a majority of students are mastering basic skills in each classroom.
Mindful Learning	__Meaningful learning experiences through field trips, project based learning and hands-on activities. __Teachers who allow for some learning through discovery through hands-on activities for subjects like scien
Thematic Instruction	__General curriculum design that incorporates school-wide themes. __Teachers who instruct through the study of themes.
Problem-solving and Logic	__Curriculum that includes specific courses in logic and/or problem-solving. __Curriculum that includes courses that encourage problem-solving, e.g. computer programming.
Arts Instruction	__Instruction in the arts (art, music, dance, theater) that is mandatory for all students, K-12.
Foreign Language Instruction	__Instruction in foreign languages that is mandatory for all students, K-12.
Technology as a Teaching and Learning Tool	__Curriculum that emphasizes using technology as a tool to solve real world problems and that offers opportunities for computer programming to all students. __Evidence that students are using technology to assist them in problem-solving, presentation, and research to solve problems. __Evidence that computers are not used only for drill and practice.

School-to-Work Programs	__School-to-Work programs to assist graduating seniors with entering the workplace. __Viable career counseling program for all students, grades 9-12. __Opportunities for students to set personal goals to develop an attitude of "big picture thinking" about the future and their roles in it.
Integrated Courses	__Curriculum that includes integrated humanities, e.g., English, art, music, history, and foreign language in coursework. __Curriculum designed so that common themes are woven through a series of classes. __Evidence that efforts are made to integrate some courses with each other, e.g., math and science for the purpose of gathering and analyzing data.
Physical Education, Movement & Dance	__Curriculum that includes regularly-scheduled physical education, movement, and/or dance courses for all students, K-12.
Communication	__Evidence that administration and teachers make it a priority to devote time to meet with parents to set goals and to solve problems regarding student placement and academic and behavioral success. __Strategies for setting student and parent goals. __Teachers who set academic goals based on state or federal standards.
Service Learning	__Specific opportunities for students to complete learning experiences in the community by providing a needed service.
Standardized Testing	__Achievement tests for the basic skills are used to measure individual student progress from the beginning to the end of the year. Scores are used to determine how to improve an individual student's instruction.

CHAPTER 6:
Physical Variables that Affect the Quality of an Education

In addition to being educated about brain-based learning and curriculum features that contribute to a quality education, parents should also realize that the physical features of a school can hamper or hasten learning. A combination of poor environmental characteristics in a school, such as an inexperienced faculty, a poorly defined classroom schedule, and a high crime rate can cause students to feel stressed. When an individual is stressed, the adrenal glands release the hormone cortisol, which can trigger physical reactions, such as increased blood pressure, depression of the immune system, and tensing of large muscles. Chronic stress, in turn, can lead to the inability to focus, and the subsequent failure to learn. In fact, physical variables, such as the ones described in this chapter, can be as important to a child's educational success as curriculum features, but the relative weight of a particular feature is ultimately determined by a parent's priority and the child's need.

Teacher-to-Student Ratios

I often tell parents that if they have to choose one outstanding variable that contributes to a quality learning environment it would be a small teacher-to-student ratio. Research on ratios has repeatedly demonstrated that students are more successful in an environment that has small teacher-to-student ratios: 15 students or less is an ideal classroom size. Where there are smaller ratios, students receive more individual attention from the teacher, and with greater attention, students feel more secure in the learning environment.

During the 1990s, federal grants were available to public

schools to hire additional teachers in grades first through third. The goal of the program was to reduce the teacher-to-student ratio to less than 1:20 for kindergarten through third grade to provide students with learning-friendly environments when they are building a foundation for their basic skills. These grants have since expired, and ratios have again crept up in many public school systems.

School Size

School size, the number of students enrolled in the school, is inversely related to a whole host of areas, such as absenteeism, violence, and poor achievement. To put it simply: as size goes up, achievement goes down. A small school of less than 250 students fosters a sense of intellectual and social intimacy that leads to satisfying personal relationships. Intimacy is a subtle but powerful variable when it comes to learning. In the book, *Creating New Schools*, author Evans Clinchy reports that in Boston and New York, after several large schools were divided into several smaller ones, there was an improvement in academic achievement. Smaller schools provide opportunities for students to succeed through the use of a greater variety of unique curriculum programs.

Related to school size is the very important variable of personal safety. Educational research has demonstrated that students who feel safe are more productive learners. Fear causes the brain to emit chemicals that prevent learning to occur. Smaller schools are safer schools because they provide an intimate community of individuals; furthermore, adults within the system can more easily identify and control inappropriate behavior.

Faculty

A school's faculty is its foundation. There is no substitute for devoted and experienced teachers. Diversity is important as well. Teachers who have a natural gift for teaching and a personal presence around students are easy to identify; although, a parent may not be able to articulate the specific behaviors that make that teacher special. In a perfect world, all schools would contain an entire faculty of individuals who fit this description.

Unfortunately, when schools remain unresponsive, isolated, and resistant to new ideas, exceptional teachers are not always welcome. In fact, idealistic teachers will not thrive in this environment. Also, in many traditional public schools, teachers earn tenure; however, tenure sometimes has little to do with the quality of an individual's teaching. While tenure gives teachers job security because the school system must maintain tenured teachers during layoffs or fill newly-vacant positions with tenured teachers, it can inhibit the school administration from filling a vacant position with the most qualified applicant. While charter schools are often able to operate outside the constraints of teacher unions and regulations regarding tenure, they may have to rely on inexperienced teachers who lack the experience to contribute to the school during the difficult and challenging circumstances that occur during its startup years.

Other faculty factors that have been identified with high performing schools include the importance of teachers examining student work and student-teacher relationships. Teacher-review of all student work – grading it relative to academic standards and communication with parents – is essential at every level of education. Overworked teachers or teachers who are not good team members, or who are not invested in making students successful, can fail to provide students with adequate or realistic feedback. Lack of feedback can lead to lack of learning. These same types of teachers are often unable to sustain positive relationships with students. An effective teacher, on the other hand, has daily lesson plans that include both the introduction of new academic skills and review of old skills, as well as a solid classroom routine that students understand and can easily follow.

In the classroom, an effective teacher should encourage both independent and collaborative learning. Academic coursework should be based on state standards, but it should also include material that is interesting and has meaning to the age group being taught. Quality teachers also include elements of brain-based learning when planning lessons. Finally, a teacher should maintain professional positive relationships with students and parents.

Parents should be aware of the effect the teaching staff has on a particular school. Teaching is a stressful profession. Some teachers improve with age, but others burn out. Teachers who are left on the payroll even though they are no longer able to perform their duties with impeccability will inhibit the learning environment of any given school. To evaluate a potential school, parents should ask the administration about its process for identifying effective teachers and its view on tenure. While observing classroom teachers, parents should use the school report card at the end of the book to identify the characteristics of a good teacher; they should also interview specific teachers and other parents whose children have been in that teacher's classroom.

Flexible Student Placement

This feature is often associated with small schools, as it requires block scheduling to be successful. Block scheduling occurs when all teachers teach the same basic skills courses at the same time. With block scheduling, students who test higher or lower on a specific basic skill can attend the class that matches their ability level. In other words, under this design, students who are advanced in one or more areas can attend the core class that challenges their learning ability. A summary of the research findings on allowing accelerated students to attend classes that match their abilities demonstrates a positive effect on student achievement that continues through college and adulthood. This particular form of acceleration also accommodates a large group of diverse learners, and I highly recommend it to parents who have the choice. Students who are forced to attend classes that are beneath their learning levels will rapidly become bored with school. I have seen first hand the detrimental effect of students who "dislike" school for this reason.

Physical Environment

As has been shown, feelings of stress can inhibit learning, and a variety of conditions can create a stressful physical environment. These include crowded conditions, fluorescent lighting, noise, an unclean and unsafe building, negative attitudes of faculty and administration, continuous viewing of a computer or video screen, and negative social situations that cannot be resolved. I am not suggesting that schools should attempt to eliminate all stress and give students their own way. Some stresses are bound to occur throughout the day. In fact, research has shown that learning to overcome obstacles is an important behavior that leads to success in life. Some stressful situations can encourage a student to learn some of the psychological skills, such as knowing when to persevere and rejecting self-pity, described by Sternberg in *Successful Intelligence*. On the other hand, sometimes situations occur that are so stressful that they affect a person's health and ability to learn. These circumstances suggest intervention and change for the student.

Governance

Schools that have autonomy over critical decisions such as scheduling, curriculum design, and assessment are schools that can be highly responsive to parents. As the executive director of the Moscow Charter School, I have experienced the effectiveness of solving problems with parents and teachers immediately; waiting for a request to go through the chain of command to a central office can be detrimentally frustrating to a parent. In a self-governing environment, parents often have greater accessibility to administrators, which means that problems can be solved on the spot. This feature should be a high priority for parents who want to work closely with their school system to design a unique program for their child.

All school administrators should be responsive to a parent whose child is having difficulty with a particular teacher. When a student has an issue with a teacher, his or her parent should try to determine if the issue is simply a personality clash or whether the teacher is unprofessional in organizing and delivering information or whether the teacher behaves unprofessionally in his or her personal relationship with the child. Even if parents believe a teacher is behaving unprofessionally, it does not pay to get angry. Instead, parents should gather information about the situation that is adversely affecting their child and find out the specific protocol to follow to file a complaint.

Technology

Technology is a highly effective and convenient classroom tool to teach thinking, problem-solving, math, writing, and organizational and research skills. It also provides a self-paced tool for the drill and practice of any subject. A number of features make up a quality technology program. Up-to-date equipment, total number of computers, adequate student-to-computer ratios, and computer literacy of the teachers are vital components of an overall program. Using technology as an eclectic tool should begin in the third grade to develop these skills for students to use in completing classroom projects.

Unfortunately, some teachers use the computer as a babysitting tool in the classroom. Excessive computer use by students in kindergarten through third grade can also take away from valuable time needed to learn basic skills, interpersonal skills, and motor skills that are so important to learn at that age. At these ages, technology can be used for drill and practice of basic skills material and strategic problem-solving, but exercises that promote staring at a video screen for extended durations should be avoided because they can damage the shape of a young child's eyes and cause vision problems. Parents should look for schools with a philosophy about technology use that takes this information into consideration.

Length of School Days and School Year

Research on longer school days and a longer school year supports more time in school to optimize learning, yet this variable has rarely been applied in public schools. The more months a student spends in school during a year, the greater the learning; this is because the large gap of two to three months during the summer when there is no instruction time is eliminated. In my opinion, pre-college students should not go for long periods of time without organized learning experiences. Much learning is lost over the summer vacation, and the first two months of the following school year are often spent playing catch-up instead of learning new material. I support a longer school year for all students but not a longer day for elementary-aged students. I believe that elementary students, and the adults teaching them, experience fatigue when the school day is too long. Fatigue is a major inhibitor to learning. However, as students get older, they are physically able to handle the rigor of longer days.

School Start and End Times

Like length of the school year and day, research has shown that school start and end times can strongly affect learning, especially for high school students. The sufficient level of melatonin, the brain chemical necessary to induce sleep, occurs later at night in teenagers than it does in children. In addition, teenagers often need eight to ten hours of sleep per night. Therefore, students in this age range often do not perform optimally during early morning classes. Some high schools across the nation have changed their starting times to 9:00 a.m. to accommodate this physiological need.

Additionally, in *Teaching With the Brain in Mind*, Eric Jenson reviews research demonstrating that our ability to retrieve information through the use of words is affected by "when" it is learned as much as by "what" is learned. According to Jenson, efficiency increases when we recall details and text in the morning and conceptual relationships in the afternoon.

Nutrition

Specific foods have been shown to be good for optimum brain functioning: green leafy vegetables, lean meats, fresh fruits and vegetables, nuts, and salmon. On the other hand, simple carbohydrates that contain sugars and saturated fats do not facilitate learning and memory. In addition, allergies to common foods such as dairy products can create behavioral and learning problems, as can dehydration.

Programs for Students with Special Needs

The federal government mandates that all public schools provide appropriate academic assistance for students who are diagnosed with a special education need. Schools are also required to provide programs for students who are advanced and labeled as gifted and talented. Once these students are tested and diagnosed by certified personnel, an Individual Education

Program (IEP) must be written to provide a plan of service. Students who are not diagnosed with special education problems, but may have deficits or delays in reading or mathematics, can also be provided with additional services. These services are unique for each school because they are determined by factors, such as the location of the school, the school's need, and its ability to apply for grants. If a child is in need of special services, the quality of these services may be a parent's most important consideration. Parents should observe and interview the special education teacher or the gifted and talented teacher; they should also interview parents of students who are already in the school's special programs.

School Tone and Atmosphere

The combination of the physical environment, teachers, and administration sets the particular tone and atmosphere for the school. Often the atmosphere can be felt immediately as one walks in the front door of a school or when communicating with the staff at the front desk. In general, a "good" atmosphere consists of happy students who are focused because they know what they are supposed to accomplish at any given moment in the school day. Students should be actively engaged in teacher or student-directed activities, but not necessarily quiet. How parents, administrators, teachers, and students (and among students themselves) communicate is also an indicator of school tone. In conversation, a positive tone of voice with a clear message indicates a pleasant atmosphere.

Physical Variables that Effect the Quality of an Education Sample Interview Questions

Most of the information in this section can be found in a school's policy manual.

– What is the school's philosophy about block scheduling for basic skills classes with placement based on achievement data, K-12?
– What is the school's procedure for serving special needs students?
– What is the school's philosophy on tenure for teachers?
– What is the administration's protocol for dealing with a parent complaint?

Physical Variables	Positive Features Schools Should Offer:
Teacher-to-Student Ratios (policy manual)	__Less than 1 to 20.
School Size (policy manual)	__Less than 250.
Faculty	__Encourages both collaborative and individual learning. __Establishes meaningful classroom routines. __Bases academic work on state standards. __Includes knowledge of brain-based learning when planning lessons. __Reviews student work and offers feedback. __Maintains professional and positive relationships with other teachers, students, and parents.
Flexible Placement for Core Academic Classes (policy manual)	__Block scheduling. __Placement of students in core classes of English, mathematics, and reading based on achievement data.
Physical Environment (policy manual)	__Clean rooms. __Adequate lighting, ventilation, and space. __Well maintained building, inside and out, e.g. shoveled sidewalks in winter. __Safe playground equipment.
Governance	__Ability to make adjustments and changes without excessive red tape. __Administration that is consistently responsive to parents.
Technology (policy manual)	__Low student-to-computer ratios for upper elementary grades and high school. __Teachers who have training or certification in educational technology as part of their teaching certificates. __Hardware that is relatively current.
Length of School Year (policy manual)	__Longer or all year is better.
Length of School Day (policy manual)	__Longer is better for secondary.

School Start & End Times (policy manual)	__Later is better in high school
Nutrition	__Lunch program offers foods that support good nutrition, such as fruits, vegetables, nuts, fish and other lean protein.
Special Education Services	__Special education teacher and other specialists, e.g., speech pathologist, counselor, and classroom aides to provide routine services. __Evaluation of students to determine qualification for special education or gifted and talented programs by certified individuals. __Formal Individualized Education Plans for students who are diagnosed with special needs.
School Tone and Atmosphere	__Positive environment resulting from the combination of teachers, administration, students, and the physical facility.

CHAPTER 7:
The Future of the Educational Experience

Unlocking a Closed Paradigm

For nearly a century, our society has been locked into an educational system characterized by eight years of grade school followed by four years of high school, and then college for those who want a professional career. Now that online education and other flexible options, such as home schooling and correspondence courses, are readily available at every level of education, this paradigm may become obsolete. Students no longer need to attend high school for four years before they enter college. Many self-paced curriculum programs, or those online programs available through virtual schools, are rapidly replacing the lock step educational programs of previous generations. With new alternatives, parents will face the challenge of planning a balanced educational program that matches the needs and goals of their children.

> With new alternatives, parents will face the challenge of planning a balanced educational program that matches the needs and goals of their children.

Today's parents are fortunate to have choices at almost every level of education, and those who take the initiative to define their own notion of academic and professional success stand a greater chance of creating an educational program for their child with which they will be satisfied. Parents will want to combine their beliefs with a data-gathering session at a potential school – as well as a good dose of logic and common sense. Parents now have opportunities to be creative with their choices to design the most successful education delivery format appropriate to their child's stage of learning. For example, grade school parents who are not happy with the course offerings of their child's school, or who have a child who has fallen behind in a course, can purchase a single curriculum course for a specific subject, or enroll the child in an online summer class or a correspondence course offered by universities throughout the nation. Upfront planning by parents can provide a wide variety of meaningful experiences for a child, and educational experiences are the means for a child to recognize and achieve their full potential. Through a wide variety of life experiences, individuals can learn to use their abilities in a balanced way.

The Politics of Accountability

Many of the common problems associated with today's public schools are the result of mandated state and federal legislation that is under-funded. While there is ample evidence to support a holistic approach to education, today's politicians are instead grappling with the notion of accountability for the nation's public school system and many schools are completely absorbed in trying to meet these regulations. While measurement of basic academic skills is necessary on a regular basis, politicians who support legislation to mandate repeated standardized testing from year to year are creating an educational environment that forces schools to teach to the test and spend valuable funding dollars on training individuals to follow complex regulations and complete excessive paperwork. Many variables are involved in making a school successful, not just its ability to teach factual information. Declaring that this form of testing actually presents a well-rounded picture of a student's intellectual strengths, as it applies to a real world environment, is a travesty, especially for individuals who have a specific learning disability or test anxiety.

Also, state and federal failure to fund public education properly has led to a gradual elimination of arts programs in many public schools. When the arts are the first to be slashed in a public school budget, both politicians and educators in administrative positions demonstrate an unfortunate cultural ignorance. By analyzing the skills that are taught through arts education, we discover that training in the arts actually enhances intellectual development and, if used properly, accelerates learning on all levels. Training in the arts makes students creatively and educationally diverse; it enhances and develops skills that help individuals function more successfully. Consistent and broad training in the arts throughout early childhood with an emphasis on creativity also enables students to become more efficient learners, thus reducing the amount of time they need for drill and practice. As a charter school founder, the reactions I have received from traditional educators to changes a charter school brings about, such as maintaining a strong arts program, provides ample evidence of some educators' disdain for teaching these soft skills; they are distrustful because they believe they are unable to assess formally the mastery of these skills.

Parents hold a great deal of power in today's educational environment and choosing a school or customizing an educational plan can be regarded as a political act. They are voting with their choices. Parents have the right to expect schools to prepare students for the real world of the 21st century. They can also control change by staying in touch with their legislators and letting them know how they feel about legislation that interferes with a local school's ability to design and manage a well-rounded curriculum.

The Pace of Change

I believe the school choice movement signals an encouraging change in American public education. Charter schools, vouchers, virtual schools, home schooling, and individual course offerings either through online or correspondence are slowly changing the content and delivery of public education and transforming the traditional mechanical educational system. Parents are driving this change. In searching for quality schools and other educational options, parents will encounter differing philosophical approaches to curriculum. They may discover that many traditional educators will be reluctant change-agents because these individuals were taught in, believe in, and practice the factory method of curriculum delivery.

The school choice movement will continue to challenge

educational systems on all levels, including many university teacher training programs. Many university teachers believe the traditional curriculum approach is the only way to teach education majors to cope with the expanding federal and state regulations for measuring K-12 student performance through standardized achievement tests.

Parents who believe they lack choice must understand that, while the pace of change seems slow, there is reason for hope, and there are alternatives. Aside from visiting schools in their area, these parents will also want to look for online credit courses, correspondence courses, or purchase a home schooling curriculum for any subject and grade that can be applied to their child's transcript in the school system. (These curriculums can now be purchased on eBay!) The movement of public education described in this book is, I believe, inevitable. Once considered merely a fad, the extensive growth of the alternative public school movement makes it the fastest, most successful structural change in public education since its inception, and educational research in how the brain learns is influencing curriculum design in many innovative schools.

> Parents who believe they lack choice must understand that, while the pace of change seems slow, there is reason for hope, and there are alternatives.

I believe that the soul of humanity is moving in a direction that will increasingly demand change in preparing our children for the workforce. When the human soul is transformed and moves into new and different territory, institutions and professionals will either move with it or be left behind. Outdated ideas will die, not because of some violent revolutionary overthrow, but because people, in this case parents, will simply withdraw their legitimacy. People will go where their collective soul leads them, toward a more comprehensive, holistic, integrated, and self-empowered approach to learning and successful intelligence.

As one who has lived in, experienced, observed, and pondered the educational system for over the past quarter century, I also sometimes feel that the pace of change is frustrating.

However, although change is sometimes agonizingly slow, the fact that there is change, which is indisputable, is encouraging. There is absolutely no doubt in my mind that educational pioneers and parents with a vision, such as those individuals who have driven the school choice movement, will be joined daily by more and more of my colleagues. There are enough educators who are sensitive and thoughtful about what really goes on within the students they are serving to acknowledge how important the brain-based approach is in education. The direction of the future in this regard is clear.

As long as education is a discipline, it will continue to grow, change, evolve, and mature, and parents will play a big part in making this happen. Human life is far too complex and mysterious for us to ever think that we have the end results all figured out. Without a dynamic synergy among professional educators to work for change, our students are paying a hefty price. If traditional educators will build a powerful bridge between the mechanisms of change and their own beliefs, many more students would be lifted out of uncertainty to experience the miraculous and exhilarating feeling of well-being that comes with fulfilling their potential.

> **Without a dynamic synergy among professional educators to work for change, our students are paying a hefty price.**

APPENDIX:
Grading Our Schools

With educated decision-making from the time your child enters kindergarten, you should have good success in choosing a school or educational program that is based on principles of success. Following these guidelines will help you achieve your goal:

1. Visit a potential school.
2. Ask the principal about the school's educational philosophy.
3. Interview the teacher of the grade your child will enter.
4. Interview parents of children who already attend the school.
5. Spend time in classrooms.
6. Ask if your child can participate in classroom activities when you visit.
7. Ask for the school policy manual and any available literature.
8. Use the following "report card" to prioritize the items that are most important to you and to formulate your questions; doing so will help you identify whether a potential school contains the criteria that create a quality learning environment.
9. Find out which on-line or correspondence courses your child's school will accept for supplementing coursework.

School Report Cards

Brain-based Learning: Sample Interview Questions

–Describe the kindergarten curriculum.

–What grade level does the school begin teaching the basic skills of reading, writing, and mathematics?

–What specialized classes does the school offer every student, including those in kindergarten?

–Does the teacher use a variety of ways, including hands-on projects to supplement work sheets and to introduce important reading, writing, and math concepts?

–Does the school or individual teachers use themes to introduce and tie together academic activities?

–What type of support specialists does the school have to assist non-traditional learners or students with learning problems?

–Describe the school and classroom schedule.

–What steps does the administration take to insure that all students will be safe on the school grounds?

–What is the school's philosophy regarding bullying and how does it respond to students who bully other students?

Brain-Based Learning Features	What a School Should Offer:
Critical Periods of Learning	__ Mastery of basic skills: reading, writing, and mathematics in grades K-6. __ Foreign language instruction beginning in kindergarten. __ Arts training, K-12, to nurture and foster creative thinking. __ Activities that promote problem-solving, e.g., hands-on math and science, K-12.
Multiple Modalities (Senses)	__ Variety of courses that use multiple senses, including art, music, physical education, dance, and theater. __ Integrated coursework, e.g., a humanities program including English, history, art, music, and foreign language tied together with a single theme.
Early Enrichment	__ Full range of enrichment courses beginning in kindergarten and extending through high school, e.g., reading, writing, arts, foreign language, physical education.
Emotion and Meaning	__ Daily lessons that include meaningful activities, simulations of real life situations, and themes, e.g., building a model to illustrate a story or a hands-on science projects.
Learning Styles	__ Flexible curriculum delivery for non-traditional learners. For example, if a child is having difficulty learning a subject through lecture and worksheets, the teacher should be willing to try another method of presentation. __ Additional professionals to serve non-traditional learners, such as supplemental reading teachers, Americorp volunteers who act as tutors, teacher's aides, speech pathologists, counselors. __ Teachers who accommodate learning styles by offering lessons that require students to perform a variety of activities for information rehearsal, e.g., student is expected to practice spelling words using a different activity for homework each night.
Relaxation, Music, Movement	__ Regularly scheduled classes in the arts and physical education.
Emotional Security	__ Safe and secure physical environment. __ Teachers who have been well trained in classroom management and can maintain a structured, positive classroom environment. __ Well-organized school and classroom schedules for students throughout the day. __ A school philosophy that minimizes violent behavior.

Curriculum Features that Support Learning: Sample Interview Questions

— How Does the No Child Left Behind Act affect the school's curriculum?

— Have courses been cut from the curriculum as a result of this legislation?

— Does the school offer a humanities program?

— Are basic skills courses offered every day at the elementary level? What time of the day are they offered?

— Is the content of the basic skills courses based on state standards?

— Is the school curriculum aligned – is it required that content flow from one grade to the other?

— How does the school use thematic learning?

— What types of specialized classes does the school offer besides basic skills courses?

— Does the curriculum include regularly-scheduled physical education classes?

— What is the school's philosophy on teaching the arts?

— What is the school's philosophy on teaching technology?

— What types of activities are included in the technology curriculum at each grade?

— What are the school's and teachers' systems for classroom management?

— Does the school offer parent/teacher conferences? How often?

— How often are report cards or progress reports sent out?

— Does the school encourage parent volunteers?

— Do administrators and teachers use test results from standardized tests to improve instruction for each student?

— Does the school offer school-to-work programs?

— What type of career counseling is available at the school?

— Does the school offer service learning programs?

Curriculum Features	What a School Should Offer:
Early Enrichment	__Curriculum that emphasizes early enrichment by offering specialty classes beginning in kindergarten. __Classes in basic skills, arts, and foreign languages starting in kindergarten.
Basic Skills: Reading, Writing and General courses	__Basic skills coursework for each grade that is based on state or national standards. __Mastery of basic skills for students in K-6, with these courses scheduled in the morning. __Curriculum in which social studies and science are offered as standard courses in all grades starting in kindergarten. __Standardized test scores for each teacher showing that a majority of students are mastering basic skills in each classroom.
Mindful Learning	__Meaningful learning experiences through field trips, project based learning and hands-on activities. __Teachers who allow for some learning through discovery through hands-on activities for subjects like science.
Thematic Instruction	__General curriculum design that incorporates school-wide themes. __Teachers who instruct through the study of themes.
Problem-solving and Logic	__Curriculum that includes specific courses in logic and/or problem-solving. __Curriculum that includes courses that encourage problem-solving, e.g., computer programming.
Arts Instruction	__Instruction in the arts (art, music, dance, theater) that is mandatory for all students, K-12.
Foreign Language Instruction	__Instruction in foreign languages that is mandatory for all students, K-12.
Technology as a Teaching and Learning Tool	__Curriculum that emphasizes using technology as a tool to solve real world problems and that offers opportunities for computer programming to all students. __Evidence that students are using technology to assist them in problem-solving, presentation, and research to solve problems. __Evidence that computers are not used only for drill and practice.

School-to-Work Programs	__School-to-Work programs to assist graduating seniors with entering the workplace. __Viable career counseling program for all students, grades 9-12. __Opportunities for students to set personal goals to develop an attitude of "big picture thinking" about the future and their roles in it.
Integrated Courses	__Curriculum that includes integrated humanities, e.g. English, art, music, history, and foreign language in coursework. __Curriculum designed so that common themes are woven through a series of classes. __Evidence that efforts are made to integrate some courses with each other, e.g., math and science for the purpose of gathering and analyzing data.
Physical Education, Movement & Dance	__Curriculum that includes regularly-scheduled physical education, movement, and/or dance courses for all students, K-12.
Communication	__Evidence that administration and teachers make it a priority to devote time to meet with parents to set goals and to solve problems regarding student placement and academic and behavioral success. __Strategies for setting student and parent goals. __Teachers who set academic goals based on state or federal standards.
Service Learning	__Specific opportunities for students to complete learning experiences in the community by providing a needed service.
Standardized Testing	__Achievement tests for the basic skills are used to measure individual student progress from the beginning to the end of the year. Scores are used to determine how to improve an individual student's instruction.

Physical Variables that Effect the Quality of an Education Sample Interview Questions

Most of the information in this section can be found in a school's policy manual.

– What is the school's philosophy about block scheduling for basic skills classes with placement based on achievement data, K-12?
– What is the school's procedure for serving special needs students?
– What is the school's philosophy on tenure for teachers?
– What is the administration's protocol for dealing with a parent complaint?

Physical Variables	Positive Features Schools Should Offer:
Teacher-to-Student Ratios (policy manual)	__Less than 1 to 20.
School Size (policy manual)	__Less than 250.
Faculty	__Encourages both collaborative and individual learning. __Establishes meaningful classroom routines. __Bases academic work on state standards. __Includes knowledge of brain-based learning when planning lessons. __Reviews student work and offers feedback. __Maintains professional and positive relationships with other teachers, students, and parents.
Flexible Placement for Core Academic Classes (policy manual)	__Block scheduling. __Placement of students in core classes of English, mathematics, and reading based on achievement data.
Physical Environment (policy manual)	__Clean rooms. __Adequate lighting, ventilation, and space. __Well maintained building, inside and out, e.g. shoveled sidewalks in winter. __Safe playground equipment.
Governance	__Ability to make adjustments and changes without excessive red tape. __Administration that is consistently responsive to parents.
Technology (policy manual)	__Low student-to-computer ratios for upper elementary grades and high school. __Teachers who have training or certification in educational technology as part of their teaching certificates. __Hardware that is relatively current.
Length of School Year (policy manual)	__Longer or all year is better.
Length of School Day (policy manual)	__Longer is better for secondary.

School Start & End Times (policy manual)	__Later is better in high school
Nutrition	__Lunch program offers foods that support good nutrition, such as fruits, vegetables, nuts, fish and other lean protein.
Special Education Services	__Special education teacher and other specialists, e.g., speech pathologist, counselor, and classroom aides to provide routine services. __Evaluation of students to determine qualification for special education or gifted and talented programs by certified individuals. __Formal Individualized Education Plans for students who are diagnosed with special needs.
School Tone and Atmosphere	__Positive environment resulting from the combination of teachers, administration, students, and the physical facility.

Bibliography

Bancroft, W.J. "Suggestopedia, Sophrology and Traditional Foreign Language Class." *Foreign Language Annals* 15 (1982): 373-379.

Brody, L.E., S.G. Stanley, and J.C. Stanley. "Five years of early entrants: Predicting successful achievement in college." *Gifted Child Quarterly*, 34, (1990) 138-142.

Byo, S.J. "Classroom Teachers' and Music Specialists' Perceived Ability to Implement the National Standards for Music Education." *Journal of Research for Music Education*, 47 (1999): 111-123.

Caine, Renate Nummela., and Geoffrey Caine. "Understanding a Brain Based Approach to Learning and Teaching." *Educational Leadership*, 28 (1990): 66-70.

_____. *Making Connections: Teaching and the Human Brain.* Alexandria, VA: Association for Supervision and Curriculum Development, 1991.

Campbell, Linda and Bruce Campbell. *Multiple Intelligences and Student Achievement: Success Stories from Six Schools.* Alexandria, VA, Association for Supervision and Curriculum Development. 1999.

Clinchy, Evans. *Creating New Schools: How Small Schools are Changing American Education.* New York, Teacher's College, 2000.

Cox, J., N. Daniel, and B.A. Boston. "*Educational Able Learners: Programs and Promising Practices.*" Austin, University of Texas Press, 1985.

Deasy, R.J., and H.M. Fulbright. "The Arts Impact on Learning." *Education Week,* November 24, 2001.

Diamond, Marian and Janet Hopson. *Magic Trees of The Mind.* New York: Penguin Putnam, Inc, 1999.

Eisner, Elliot, "Ten Lessons the Arts Teach," in *Learning and the Arts: Crossing Boundaries* (Los Angeles: Amdur Spitz & Associates, 2000), 9-14.

Fiske, Edward B. *Champions of Change: The Impact of the Arts of Learning.* Arts Education Partnership and the President's Committee on the Arts and Humanities, 1999. <http://www.aep-arts.org/PDF%20Files/ChampsReport.pdf>.

Gardner, Howard. *Frames of Mind.* New York: Basic Books, 1983.

_____. *Multiple Intelligences.* New York: Basic Books, 1993.

_____. *The Disciplined Mind.* New York: Simon and Schuster, 1999.

Goleman, Daniel. *Emotional Intelligence.* New York: Bantam Books, 1995.

Hanson, H.P., "Twenty-five years of Advanced Placement Programs: Encouraging able students." *The College Board Review,* (1980) 35, 8-13.

Heath, Shirley B., *Living the Arts Through Language + Learning: A Report on Community-Based Youth Organizations.* Americans for the Arts, 1998.

Hedges, W.D. "At what age should children enter the first grade? A comprehensive review of research." Ann Arbor, Michigan, University Microfilms International, 1977.

Huffman, Molly and Julie Powell. *School Choices in Greater Portland.* Portland, OR: TACT, 1996.

Jensen, E.P. *The Learning Brain.* Del Mar, CA: Turning Point for Teachers, 1994.

_____. *Super-Teaching*. Del Mar, CA: Turning Point for Teachers, 1988.

Kirk, R.E. *Experimental Design: Procedures for the Behavioral Sciences*. Pacific Grove, CA: Brooks/Cole Publishing, 1995.

Kulilk, I.A. and C.C. Kulik. "Synthesis of research on effects of accelerated instruction." *Educational Leadership* 42, (1984) 84-89.

Langer, Ellen. *The Power of Mindful Learning*. New York: Addison-Wesley Company, Inc., 1997.

Lozanov, G. *Suggestology and Outlines of Suggestopedy*. New York: Gordon & Breach, 1978.

Maxwell, John. *Thinking for Change: 11 Ways Highly Successful People Approach Life and Work*. Nashville: Warner Faith, 2003.

Morse, D. *Whole Schools Initiative Evaluation Summary*. Mississippi Arts Commission, 1998.

National Center for Education Statistics, Institute of Education Sciences, U.S. Dept of Education. NGA Center for Best Practices, 2002.

Ostrander, Sheila, and Lynn Schroeder. *Supermemory, the Revolution*. New York: Carroll & Graf, 1991.

Papert, Seymour. *Mindstorms: Children, Computers and Powerful Ideas*. Cambridge, MA: Perseus Publishing, 1993.

_____. *The Connected Family*. Atlanta, GA: Longstreet Press, 1996.

Paul, Richard, and Linda Elder.*Critical Thinking: Tools for Taking Charge of Your Learning and Your Life*. Prentice Hall, 2001.

Pratt, David. *Curriculum: Design and Development*. New York, Harcourt Brace Jovanovich, 1980.

President's Committee on the Arts and Humanities and The Arts Education Partnership. *Gaining the Arts Advantage: Lessons from School Districts that Value Arts Education*, 1999. <http://www.pcah.gov/gaa/index.html.>

Progressive Policy Institute. "Building Skills for the New Economy," *Policy Report*, April 2001.

Rose, Colin. *Accelerated Learning*, New York: Dell Publishing, 1987.

Rural Information Center. "Innovative Approaches in Rural Education." *Rural Information Publication Series*, No. 72, 2000.

Saterfiel, T.H., and Joyce McLarty. "Assessing Employability Skills." ERIC Digest, Educational Resources Information Center, 1995. <http://ericae.net/db/edo/ED391109.htm.>

Schroeder, Lynn, and Sheila Ostrander. *Superlearning*. New York, Dell, 1981.

Sternberg, Robert J. *Successful Intelligence*. New York: Penguin Putnam Inc., 1997.

Winner, E., and L. Hetland. "Does Studying the Arts Enhance Academic Achievement?" *Education Week*, November 1, 2000.

Index

A

B

C

D

E

F

G

H

I

Notes:

Notes:

ISBN 141205640-3

9 781412 056403